Narrow Gauge Railroading in the San Juan Triangle

The Rio Grande Southern, the Ouray Branch of the D&RG and Otto Mears' Silverton RR

Ridgway Railroad Museum
PO Box 588
Ridgway, CO 81432

ISBN-13: 978-1985134140
ISBN-10: 19855134144

Editor
Don Paulson

Authors
Thomas Hillhouse
Rodney Holloway
Bonnie Koch
Keith Koch
Don Paulson
Jim Pettengill
Karl Schaeffer

Layout Design
Don Paulson

Cover Design
Gary Coyne

Cover Photos
Front cover photos: SRR right of way (Don Paulson); D&RGW Caboose 0575 (Don Paulson); D&RGW No. 315 (Jim Pettengill); Re-created RGS Motor No. 1 (Don Paulson); RGS Trout Lake Water Tank (Don Paulson). Back cover photo: Authors on D&RGW Caboose 0575 Platform (Don Paulson).

Published by

First two printings published by Mt. Sneffels Press, P.O. Box 98, Ridgway, CO 81432

Third printing published by Createspace, an Amazon Company.

Preface

In the summer of 2005 the Ridgway Railroad Museum approached David Mullings, the editor and owner of *The Ouray Plaindealer* and The *Ridgway Sun,* with a proposal to write semi-monthly columns for these two newspapers on topics relating to the narrow gauge railroading history of Ouray County. David agreed and the first article was published in the *Ouray Plaindealer* in October of 2005. Over the past three and a half years more than 40 of these articles have now been published.

The authors of these articles, who are all active members of the Ridgway Railroad Museum, include **Tom Hillhouse** (retired corporate attorney and Vice president of the Ouray County Historical Society), **Rodney Holloway** (Ridgway Railroad Museum volunteer and too young to retire), **Bonnie Koch** (retired elementary teacher and Ridgway Railroad Museum Educational Coordinator), **Keith Koch** (retired high school teacher and National Model Railroad Association Master Modeler), **Don Paulson** (retired college professor and Curator of the Ouray County Museum), **Jim Pettengill** (retired geologist and freelance writer), and **Karl Schaeffer** (retired railroad mechanical engineer and President of the Ridgway Railroad Museum).

This book is a compilation of most of these newspaper articles, which have been edited from their original versions. Appropriate historic photos, contemporary photos, maps and railroad forms accompany the articles.

I would like to thank Keith Koch and Beth Paulson for their editorial assistance; Karl Schaeffer for his advice on all aspects of the book; David Mullings of the Ouray County Newspapers for first publishing these articles; Pat Davarn of the Ouray County Newspapers for suggesting that we publish these articles in book form; the Board of the Ridgway Railroad Museum for their support in this project; the Ouray County Historical Society, The Colorado Historical Society, the Ridgway Railroad Museum and Cornelius Hauck for use of the photos appearing in this book; and Dave Casler owner of Mt. Sneffels Press. I am also appreciative of the time and effort expended by the authors of the articles appearing in this book.

Don Paulson
Editor
Ouray, Colorado
April 2009

Table of Contents

Introduction

Part of the mission of the Ridgway Railroad Museum is to provide educational material about the narrow gauge railroads that played such an important role in the development of Ouray County and southwestern Colorado. The Museum focuses on the three railroads that served Ouray County: the Ouray Branch of the Denver and Rio Grande (Western) Railroad, the Rio Grande Southern Railroad, and the Silverton Railroad.

Most railroads use signs, called Mile Posts (MP), that are posted at every mile on the right of way indicating the number of miles from a set starting point. On the Rio Grande Southern, Ridgway was located at MP 00 with Rico at MP 66.24 and Durango at MP 162.60. On the Silverton Railroad MP 00 was Silverton and for the D&RG narrow gauge MP 00 was Denver. Engineers used the mileposts to determine their train speed by measuring the time between mile markers using their railroad-approved watches. The mileposts were also used to indicate a location in case of track damage, a wreck, etc. Many of the articles refer to a specific milepost along the right of way.

In order for the reader to better appreciate the articles that follow, a short history of each of these railroads is presented in this introduction.

Rio Grande Southern south of Trout Lake. *Wolford Collection, Ridgway Railroad Museum.*

Ouray Branch of the Denver and Rio Grande (Western) Railroad[1]

General William Jackson Palmer established the Denver and Rio Grande Railroad (D&RG) in 1871. It was planned to connect Denver with Mexico City but after confrontations in southern Colorado with the Santa Fe Railroad, Palmer headed west from Pueblo through the Royal Gorge to reach the mines of Aspen and Leadville.

Eventually, Palmer extended the road through Salida, Gunnison, Montrose and Grand Junction to the Utah border where it met his D&RGW railroad from Salt Lake City. He also built an extension into the San Juan Mountains through Alamosa and Durango to Silverton. Palmer had seen narrow gauge railroads in Wales and was convinced that it would be much cheaper to build his railroad narrow gauge (three-feet between the rails) in mountains where extensive rockwork, excavation and sharp curves would be required. By 1889 the D&RG had more than 1700 miles of narrow gauge track. In 2009 only the 50 miles from Durango to Silverton and the 80 miles from Antonito, Colorado to Chama, New Mexico remained.

The narrow gauge rails reached Montrose, Colorado in 1882 but the branch line 30 miles south to Ouray was not constructed until 1886-1887 (see map on page 8). The arrival of the railroad resulted in increased prosperity for Ouray, and most of the city's prominent Victorian commercial buildings were constructed in the first few years after the railroad was extended into Ouray. The D&RG branch originally had a station at Dallas about half way between Montrose and Ouray. The Town of Ridgway was not founded until four years later with the construction of Otto Mears' Rio Grande Southern Railroad.

The movement of ore out of Ouray and supplies into Ouray as well as passenger service ensured that the branch would prosper well into the 20th century. The depression of the 1930s took a toll on the railroad and the town. Passenger service ended in 1936 and the beautiful Ouray depot burned in 1948. The rails were removed from Ouray to Ridgway in 1953, and the remaining Ridgway to Montrose section was standard gauged. This route lasted two more decades until low traffic and the impending construction of the Ridgway Dam forced abandonment in 1976.

---

[1] For a history of the Ouray Branch of the D&RG see: Chappell, Gordon, "Train Time in Ouray;" in Hauck, C. W., Ed., *Colorado Rail Annual No. 11*, Colorado Railroad Museum, Golden, CO, 1973.

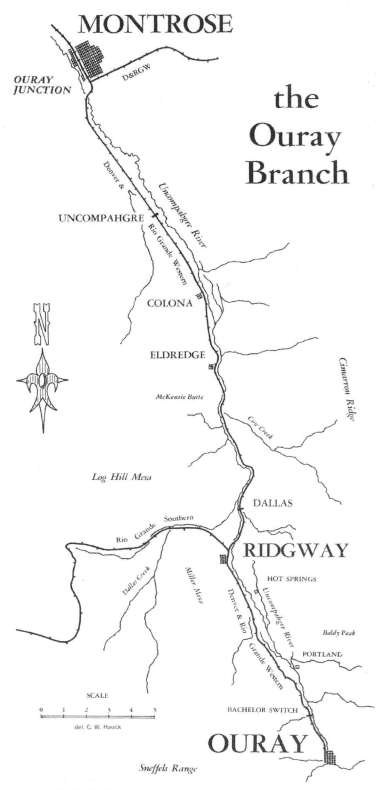

D&RG Ouray Branch Map, *Cornelius Hauck*

Rio Grande Southern Railroad[2]

The narrow gauge Rio Grande Southern Railroad (RGS) was built in 1890-91 by Otto Mears in order to tap the mineral wealth in the mines surrounding Telluride, Ophir and Rico, Colorado as well as provide transportation for the communities lying between Ridgway and Durango, Colorado (see page 10 for a map). Mears built numerous toll roads and several railroads in the San Juan Mountains of southwestern Colorado and was known during his lifetime as the "Pathfinder of the San Juans."[3]

The northern terminus, railroad shops and the administrative offices were located in a new town called Ridgway, named after Robert Ridgway who was construction superintendent for the northern half of the RGS. The construction was financed partly through the enormous profits provided to Mears by the Silverton Railroad.

The D&RG relocated its right of way to meet the RGS at Ridgway, which resulted in the rather quick demise of Dallas as the merchants moved their businesses to the new town. The railroad was completed only two years before the Silver Panic of 1893, and it went into receivership which resulted in Mears losing control of the RGS. For the next 30 years the RGS was the poor stepchild of the D&RG railroad.

The D&RG lost control of the RGS in 1929 when Victor Miller was appointed as receiver. Miller put the railroad back on a financially sounder basis with many innovations. The RGS was in danger of losing the lucrative mail contract, but they could not afford to run two passenger trains requiring five crewmen each and many tons of coal. Miller had Jack Odenbaugh build RGS Motor No. 1 in 1931 in which a single motorman and a few gallons of gasoline replaced an expensive steam train. The motor paid for itself in less than a month. The railroad built a total of seven motors in the next five years and they kept the railroad running for two more decades.

The railroad ran annual fall stock rushes to move cattle and sheep to market. At one time Placerville, Colorado had the second largest livestock loadings in Colorado. In addition, the RGS served the mines above Telluride and Rico, the coal mines near Durango, and the lumber mills near Dolores. In February of 1949 the water level in

---

[2] For a comprehensive history of the RGS see: Coleman, Ross, McCoy, Dell A., *et.al. The RGS Story, Volumes I-XII*, Sundance Publications, Denver, CO, 1990-2006

[3] For biographies of Mears see: Tucker, Eva F., *Otto Mears and the San Juans*, Western Reflections Publishing Company, Montrose, CO, 2003; Kaplan, Michael, *Otto Mears Paradoxical Pathfinder*, San Juan County Book Company, Silverton, CO 1982.

Rotary No. 2 was allowed to run low and the boiler exploded. No funds were available to rebuild the rotary, and without a means to clear snow blockades, the railroad was severely crippled.

The RGS lost the mail contract in 1950 and in the spring of 1950 converted four of the motors to Galloping Geese for hauling tourists. The tourist operation lasted 18 months but did not provide enough income to keep the railroad solvent. The receiver filed for abandonment in December of 1951 with final approval for abandonment coming in April of 1952.

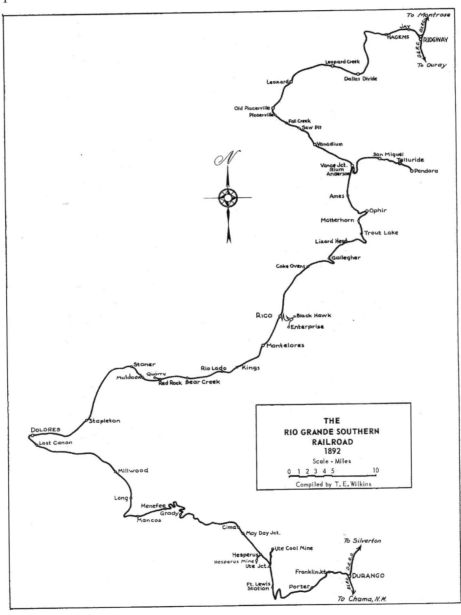

RGS System Map. *Colorado Railroad Museum Collection.*

Silverton Railroad[1]

The narrow gauge Silverton Railroad (SRR) was built in 1887-88 by Otto Mears to reach the fabulously rich mines of the Red Mountain Mining District lying on either side of Red Mountain Pass between Ouray and Silverton, Colorado (see map on page 12). In 1887 the rails were laid from Silverton to Burro Bridge, the current location of the Ophir Pass turn off on U.S. Highway 550.

In the spring of 1888 Mears hired Charles Gibbs to complete the railroad. Gibbs employed 400 Navajo Indians and Mexicans and built the railroad from Burro Bridge over 11,113 foot Red Mountain Pass and down into Ironton in less than eight months! In 1889 the railroad was extended to the Albany Smelter in Ironton Park. Gibbs built three engineering marvels on this 20-mile railroad: the Chattanooga Loop on the south side of Red Mountain Pass; the station within a wye at Red Mountain Town; and the Corkscrew Gulch Turntable, which is said to be the only turntable ever constructed on the main line of a railroad in the United States.

During its first three years of existence the Silverton Railroad was the most profitable railroad, mile per mile, in the United States. The rich silver mines served by the Silverton Railroad included the Yankee Girl, Guston, Robinson, Paymaster, National Belle, and Silver Bell. The Silver Panic of 1893 resulted in the closing of most of the mines on Red Mountain but Mears was able to remain in control of the railroad. In 1904 he leased the Silverton Railroad to a group of associates from Silverton who cut the railroad back to the Joker Tunnel above Ironton and replaced the original 30-pound rail with 45-pound rail. For many years the only shipper on the railroad was the Silver Ledge Mill on the east end of the Chattanooga Loop. That mill burned in 1914 and very little rail service occurred after that time. The railroad was abandoned in the early 1920s and the rail was ripped up in 1926.

Today one can walk on most of the right-of-way of the Silverton Railroad. Every September during their Ouray County Railroad Days, the Ridgway Railroad Museum gives guided hikes of almost the entire roadbed of the Silverton Railroad (see the Museum website for details: www.ridgwayrailroadmuseum.org).

---

[1] For more information about the Silverton Railroad and the other two Mears railroads that radiated out of Silverton see: Sloan, Robert E., and Skowronski, Carl E., *The Rainbow Route*, Sundance Publications, Silverton, CO, 1975; Smith, P. David, *Mountains of Silver*, Pruett Publishing Company, Boulder, CO, 1994.

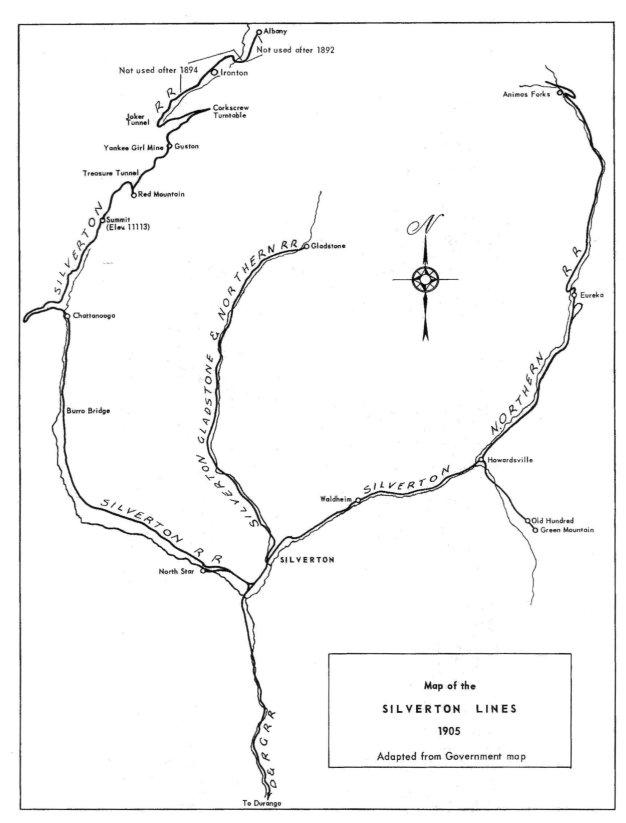

Map of the railroads radiating out of Silverton. *Colorado Railroad Museum Collection.*

Dreams and Historical Preservation
Bonnie Koch

One could say that Bob Richardson founded not only the Colorado Railroad Museum, but the Ridgway Railroad Museum as well.

In the 1950s when the Rio Grande Southern was seeing its demise, Bob discovered several boxes of materials that were headed for the dump. He gathered them up and handed them over to Ridgway resident Smiles C. Dunn with the admonition, "Keep these in a safe place. Some day there will be a museum here to celebrate the contribution of the Rio Grande Southern to southwestern Colorado."

In 1998, almost fifty years later, the Ouray County Historical Society began exploring the possibility of developing a branch to recognize the ranching and railroad history of Ridgway. Austin Baer, then a Ridgway resident, attended the initial meetings and was instrumental in eventually establishing an independent railroad Museum in Ridgway – fulfilling Bob Richardson's prophecy. Austin became the first Ridgway Railroad Museum Board President.

In the short few years of its existence, the Museum has made significant contributions to the preservation of Colorado Railroad history. With a focus on restoration, education and research its members have developed a valuable resource for anyone from 6 to 96 who is interested in how railroads impacted and changed life on the Western Slope. In 2008 alone, there were 7,084 visitors served by the Museum from 46 states and 15 foreign countries. Museum membership consists of people from throughout the U.S. and England - historians, RGS buffs, model railroaders and those who take pride in knowing that Ridgway started life as a railroad town.

Restoration has been at the forefront during our existence. Karl Schaeffer began it with his meticulous re-creation of Jack Odenbaugh's Motor No. 1 which is now available for visitors to ride, experiencing the joy of stepping back in time 75 years. In 2006 D&RGW Caboose 0575 was moved from the city park in Ouray and brought back to life with historical accuracy. In May of 2008, Galloping Goose No. 4 was transported from Telluride to Ridgway where it is now going through a multi-year rebuilding that will bring it back to the year 1951.

A railroad museum exists to educate the public about railroads. Our artifacts and materials have provided the background for museum members to give presentations sponsored by the Ouray County Historical Society, the Telluride Historical Society, the Montrose County Historical Society, National Narrow Gauge Conventions, and the Ridgway State Park. Members write bimonthly articles on railroad history for the *Ouray County Plaindealer* and the *Ridgway Sun* newspapers as well as the monthly Museum newsletter. As of this date, almost 1,000 children in Ouray, San Miguel and Montrose Counties have received instruction either at the museum or through classroom visits. We have developed lessons that work with the state mandated Colorado history unit taught in 3rd or 4th grade and our members make annual visits sponsored by the Ouray County Historical Society to present these lessons to several schools.

Research and organization of RGS information into a useable database is an ongoing goal of the Museum. Initially, using the materials that Bob Richardson rescued as well as other donations, we began culling facts into researchable topics such as a list of RGS Train Delays, identification of all the RGS engines and telegram communications. One of our biggest projects to date has been the compilation of RGS employees, identifying them by name, position, pay, years of service and where Museum information about them is located. There are presently more than 2,000 individuals identified. The information is available on our website, www.ridgwayrailroadmuseum.org and at the Museum itself.

In the spring of 2008 the Colorado Railroad Museum in Golden donated box loads of additional paper resources about the RGS. Materials ranged from "personal records," to train registers, to cancelled checks, to correspondence about purchases and shipments. Since then, Museum members have spent hundreds of hours going through each box, identifying what is in them, shaking out the dirt, and putting them into new packaging if needed. Information gathered while just perusing the papers has already provided many recent newspaper and Museum newsletter articles. The list of RGS employees has increased dramatically as we discover new personnel regularly or more facts about those previously identified.

Our next goal is to combine our resources so that information is in a quickly obtainable format. Checks need to go together in chronological order. Correspondence needs to be easily identified by year, location on the railroad or author. These valuable documents, some of which are well over 100 years old, need to be stored in a manner that will keep them in good condition for another 100 years. When we receive requests asking for copies of materials that relate to a particular person, we need to be able to go to that material with some ease and answer that request. The Museum also responds to inquiries for information from the model railroad community.

Ridgway was where the Rio Grande Southern began its journey up and over Dallas Divide to service the mining communities of Telluride, Ophir, and Rico and on to Durango, providing a link to two sections of the Denver & Rio Grande. Ridgway serviced the engines in its roundhouse and provided the offices to conduct everyday business. It is appropriate that the Ridgway Railroad Museum should also now house some of the historical information that documents the rise and fall of the Rio Grande Southern. In a short nine years, the Museum has developed a proven track record (no pun intended) that shows that not only does it value railroad preservation, but it capably contributes to it as well.

Ridgway was the starting point of Otto Mears' dream. A Ridgway Railroad Museum was the forethought of Bob Richardson when he left those first boxes for safekeeping. As part of Western Slope history, Ridgway will always be the home of the Rio Grande Southern Railroad. In partnership with the Colorado Railroad Museum, it will also maintain both of those visions for future generations.

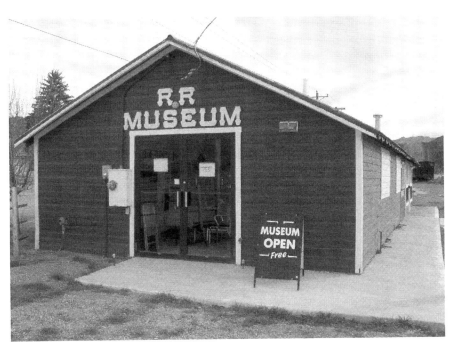

Ridgway Railroad Museum. *Photo by Keith Koch.*

The Railroad Cars at the Ridgway Railroad Museum

On the display track at the Ridgway Railroad Museum are five examples of the types of narrow gauge cars that operated on the Ouray Branch of the Denver and Rio Grande and the Rio Grande Southern Railroad headquartered in Ridgway, Colorado.

Each of these cars has a unique history, and each was designed to haul specific items. A limited number of these railroad cars still exist. When cars reached the end of their useful life, they were often scrapped for their metal parts. Burning the wooden shells and recovering the remaining metal accomplished this.

While these cars are typical examples of narrow gauge rolling stock, there are several other types of cars, which are not part of our current collection. Among these are tank cars, refrigerator cars, flatcars, combines and passenger cars. If the opportunity were to present itself, the Museum would consider additional acquisitions.

Ridgway Railroad Museum. *Photo by Don Paulson.*

D&RG(W) Boxcar 3130
Karl Schaeffer

This is one of 750 cars built for the D&RG in 1904 at a cost of $708.50 per car by the American Car and Foundry of St. Louis. They were equipped with 26-inch wheels, were 30 feet long and had a capacity of 25 tons. A boxcar hauled a variety of freight and was the rolling stock of choice for hauling many commodities. In southwestern Colorado these cars, in addition, hauled gold and silver ore. A boxcar was not open to the elements and could be locked for security reasons. Because of the weight of the ore, it could only be loaded over the trucks (wheels) of the cars. The loading and unloading of boxcars required a lot of manual labor and sometimes shovels. These narrow gauge boxcars were used in the Ridgway area until 1953.

Boxcar 3130 was rebuilt at Alamosa in 1926. It had new roof beams, a new 'Murphy' roof, and body bolsters applied. In the spring of 2000 boxcar 3130 was moved from Colona back to Ridgway where the Ridgway Railroad Museum started its restoration with financial assistance from the National Railroad Historical Society and Ridgway Community Pride. Trucks were donated by the D&SNG, and it was painted and stenciled properly. By researching "Cars on Hand" documents we have a record of boxcar 3130 being on the Rio Grande Southern Railroad in 1935 and 1938.

D&RGW Boxcar 3130. *Photo by Don Paulson.*

D&RG(W) Stockcar 5574
Karl Schaeffer

In 1904 the American Car and Foundry of St. Louis, Missouri built 350 stockcars for the Denver and Rio Grande Railroad at a cost of $689.99 each. They were equipped with 26-inch wheels, were 30 feet long and had a capacity of 25 tons. Stockcar 5574 was built to haul sixteen cattle. Other stockcars were double decked for hauling forty sheep. Shippers were known to load many more livestock than this! The story is told that a "Judas" goat was used to lead the sheep into the stockcars. Placerville, on the RGS route, was once the second busiest stock shipping point on the Colorado narrow gauge railroad system.

Fall was known as the "stock rush" when every available stockcar was put into service to move cattle and sheep to market. Federal laws regulate the treatment of livestock transported on railroads. Regulations cover how many hours they can be transported before they have to be fed and watered. Once stockcars were loaded, the railroad moved livestock over the rails with highest priority.

Stockcar 5574 received Safety Appliance updates in February 1914 and was rebuilt at Alamosa, Colorado in April 1926. At that time it was repainted black from the original reddish brown, was re-stenciled, had new roof beams, roof, and body bolsters applied. The narrow gauge lines of the D&RG and Rio Grande Southern used stockcars in the Ridgway area until 1953. Stockcar 5574 was retired under AFE (Authorization for Expenditure) 7575 in December of that year. 1970 D&RGW records show it as "lost". It was later found in the Alamosa yards and sold to a scrap dealer who was dismantling these types of cars for scrap iron.

Wayne Kinzie of Alva, OK rescued D&RGW 5574 from the torch. In the summer of 1999 it was purchased by the Ridgway Railroad Museum and moved back to Ridgway where it was restored to its1950s appearance. The car was first spotted on e-Bay and had a non-prototypical green coat of paint. The stockcar was rolled onto a badly overloaded 7-ton hay trailer to be pulled by a 1-ton truck. The stockcar which weighs about 11 tons was too much for the trailer, causing seven blowouts on the return trip to Ridgway. At the Museum, roof beams were repaired, it was painted black, stenciled properly, and the 'A' end sill was replaced. We have a "Cars on Hand" report, which documents that D&RGW 5574 operated on the RGS.

D&RGW Stock Car 5574. *Photo by Don Paulson.*

D&RG(W) Drop Bottom Gondola 702
Karl Schaeffer

Drop bottom gondola 702 was built in 1904 at a cost of $849.56 by the National Car Company (later ACF) for the Denver and Rio Grande Railroad. It is 30 feet long, has a capacity of 25 tons and is equipped with 26-inch wheels. It was one of 100 such cars. It was built with bottom dump doors for rapid unloading at D&RG locomotive coal facilities built for this purpose. On the RGS, drop bottoms would have been unloaded by hand with a shovel. They were built to haul coal, dirt and gravel (for ballast) on the narrow gauge lines of the D&RG and Rio Grande Southern. Gondola 702 was rebuilt in 1918. It had a new door operating system installed and the capacity was increased. Note that currently the stenciling is different on the two sides of the car. The north side lettering was used after 1939. The south side lettering (shown in the photo below) was used from 1926 until about 1939. Gondola 702 was acquired in 2004 from the Durango and Silverton Narrow Gauge Railroad and moved to the Ridgway Railroad Museum from Durango. The major restoration on the drop bottom has been replacing of the doors. To this point we have not located any "Cars on Hand" reports showing #702 on the RGS and have found no 700 series gondolas that operated north of Mancos on the RGS.

D&RGW Drop Bottom Gondola 702. *Photo by Don Paulson.*

D&RG 04914, A Boxcar Converted To An Outfit Car
Karl Schaeffer and Don Paulson

D&RG boxcar 4914 was built in 1896 at the cost of $545.00 by the Ohio Falls Car Manufacturing Company in Jeffersonville, Indiana. It had link and pin couplers and a "straight air" brake system. The link and pin system was very dangerous and resulted in many missing fingers and some deaths. In 1903 the car received Westinghouse Automatic Airbrakes and automatic "knuckle" type couplers as required by federal regulations.

When the D&RG acquired new boxcars, D&RG 4914 was transformed into an outfit car at which time it was re-numbered 04914, an indication that it was now a non-revenue car. As an outfit car it was the mobile home of a D&RG Water Service Supervisor and his family. The car would be moved to locations on the railroad where repairs on water tanks were needed. The car had an icebox and a coal-burning stove for both warmth and cooking. It was common for the wife of the Supervisor to prepare meals for the water service crew.

The Museum also acquired the outfit car from the Durango and Silverton Railroad in 2004. Both the outfit car and the drop bottom gondola were moved from Durango to the Museum by a semi pulling a lowboy trailer. It traveled on Highway 550 over Molas, Coal Bank and Red Mountain Passes.

According to Silverton resident Fritz Klinke, work car 04914 has quite a history. Writing in the November 2004 issue of the *Colorado Time Table*, Mr. Klinke reveals that the car once sat on a short piece of track at Gato/Pagosa Junction on the D&RGW and was scheduled to be burned in place in the early 1960s to salvage the scrap iron. Before this it may have served as a temporary station.

According to Klinke, "Conductor Punk Blackstone heard of this [plans to burn the car] and purchased the car from the railroad for $50, which was the going disposal price for car bodies. Punk then arranged for the car to get back on the siding, and on one of his trips through with a freight train, they chained the car to the tail end of the caboose and pulled it into Durango."

Klinke provides several other stories of ownership transfers and attempts to move the car, finishing with "the car has a continuous draft gear and wheels cast at the

Fort Dodge, Iowa something or other. It may be the sole surviving example of the continuous draft gear car around – that I'm not sure about."

Another account has the water service supervisor continually moving "his" car around on the D&RGW railroad to prevent the car from being painted "maintenance of way grey." If this is true, it is another feature that makes car 04914 unique.

The Museum has replaced all of the windows and doors and installed a new roof. One end of the car has been restored to its original straight air, and link-and-pin coupler configuration. Waffle board has been installed on the inside walls on the eastern end of the car. The interior walls were painted the original blue-gray-green color, while the ceiling is its original institutional tan. An inspection window was left so visitors can see the original interior wall. Some of the bead board style interior roofing boards have also been replaced.

The work car was returned to a water service car in 2007. Inside the car there is a photo exhibit of all RGS and several D&RGW narrow gauge water tanks as well as interpretive information about water service on the Colorado narrow gauge railroads. Work car 04914 presently is open for public inspection, and also has display items from RGS Motor No. 4.

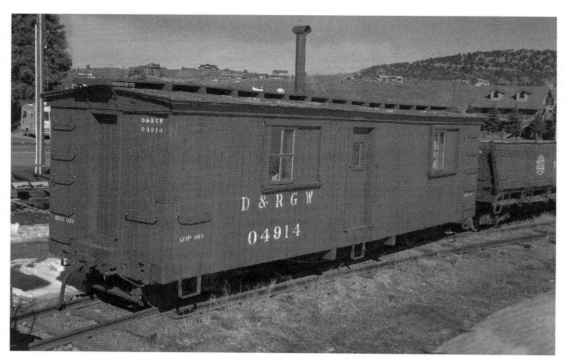

D&RGW Work Car 04914. *Photo by Don Paulson.*

D&RG(W) Narrow Gauge Caboose 0575
Don Paulson

Cabooses were one of the most important pieces of non-revenue rolling stock on a railroad. They were equipped with an icebox for food storage, a water cooler, and a coal burning stove for cooking and warmth. There were bunks for sleeping and storage for tools.

The caboose also was the conductor's office on the road and his home away from home in the event that his train was snowbound somewhere on the line. While the engineer and fireman operated the locomotive, it was the conductor who was in charge of the train. On the D&RG, and many other railroads, it often worked out that the conductor would be assigned one caboose for an extended period of time, and conductors developed a sense of ownership of "their" caboose.

Denver and Rio Grande Western Railroad Caboose 0575 was built in Denver in June of 1886 at the Burnham Shops of the Denver and Rio Grande Railroad. It operated all over the D&RG (D&RGW after 1921) narrow gauge lines. The D&RG narrow gauge cabooses were always individuals with no two alike except when a class was first built. The most knowledgeable expert on these cabooses is Robert Sloan who has divided them into five classes. Caboose 0575 is one of 15 class 2 cabooses built between 1886 and 1890. Caboose 0575 was significantly rebuilt in the Alamosa car shops in the mid-1920s. During its active lifetime on the D&RGW (1921-1953) it was used mostly on the old Third Division between Salida and Montrose, Colorado. Attempts have been made to document its presence in Ouray but, unfortunately, most of the Ouray train register records were destroyed in 1948 when the Ouray Depot burned and the remaining files at Montrose were also destroyed when the branch was abandoned in 1953.

When the D&RGW began to abandon their narrow gauge lines in the 1950s they donated a number of cabooses to Colorado towns that were served by the narrow gauge. Caboose 0575 was donated to the City of Ouray in June of 1953. On April 6, 1953 it arrived in Montrose on a standard gauge flat car and, although the narrow gauge tracks were still intact from Ridgway to Ouray, there was no narrow gauge motive power to bring it to Ouray. On April 18th it was trucked to Ouray on a lowboy provided by the Colorado Highway Department and using a winch truck rented from the

D&RGW, the caboose was placed on Main Street south of the Beaumont Hotel where the Ago Gallery is currently located. The caboose was used as the Chamber of Commerce information booth until 1977 when the Chamber moved to a building at the swimming pool. In September of 1977 Ouray County moved the caboose to a location at the south end of the swimming pool parking lot. At some point the City of Ouray donated the caboose to the Ouray County Historical Society.

In June of 2006, under a agreement between the Ouray County Historical Society and the Ridgway Railroad Museum, the caboose was moved from the park in Ouray to the Museum where it under went yet another major restoration. The caboose had seriously deteriorated over the last 13 years with the end sills and roofing being the most serious problems. Museum members re-sided, replaced the roof, installed new windows, window glass, windowsills, rebuilt the end platforms, and the end sills of the caboose. Caboose 0575 is a favorite of Museum visitors as it is open during Museum hours to view its interior.

D&RGW Caboose 0575, November 2007. *Photo by Don Paulson.*

Ouray Caboose Restoration
Don Paulson

The Ouray caboose, D&RGW 0575, has been stabilized and partly restored several times since coming to Ouray in 1953. In 1979, Bill Jones of Silverton supervised extensive repairs to the caboose with the goal of preventing further water damage. The caboose was painted in its original red color and 1886 lettering style. In 1991 to 1993 the Ouray Woman's Club funded an extensive restoration. At this time a decision was made to return the caboose to its appearance as of 1953, the last year of D&RGW service to Ouray. The interior was stripped of paint and repainted the light pea green that is presently there. Seats and mattresses were recovered with black Naugahyde. At this time window glass was replaced with Plexiglas in an attempt to prevent vandalism. The exterior was repainted and stenciled to the appropriate 1953 lettering.

The caboose significantly deteriorated over the next 13 years with the end sills and roofing being the most serious problems and needing immediate attention. There were also a number of other major structural problems.

In 2005 a grant was obtained from the Colorado Historical Society to evaluate the damage and delineate the needed repairs. Through an agreement worked out by Tom Hillhouse, then OCHS President, and Karl Schaeffer, Ridgway Railroad Museum (RRM) President, the RRM agreed to undertake the major repairs needed.

D&RGW Caboose 0575 is a uniquely important artifact of the railroad history of Ouray County. The Boards of both OCHS and RRM unanimously agreed that moving the caboose to Ridgway was in the best interest of the caboose and the people of Ouray County. The agreement provided for a prominent plaque acknowledging the financial contributions of The Ouray Woman's Club, The Massard Foundation and the Citizens of Ouray. On May 30, 2006 the caboose was moved from the park in Ouray to the Ridgway Railroad Museum where it has been restored using the D&RGW guidelines for narrow gauge caboose repair.

One of the more difficult tasks in the restoration was removal of hundreds of nut and bolt castings from the car. More than 50 years of rust made it necessary to cut off some of the bolts. Several months of soaking in oil allowed about half of the nuts to be removed with a wrench while the others needed to be cut off. All of the safety railing had to be removed in order to replace the siding. This was also difficult because the bolts were peened over for safety. A moto tool was used to cut the end of the bolt off so that the nuts could be removed.

All of the windows were replaced using the old windows as templates. Both end sills were removed and replaced. Each new fir end sill needed to have more than 30 accurately drilled holes to attach all of the hardware. D&RGW rules allow the end, intermediate and side sills to be spliced but not the center sills. Fortunately, most of the damage was in the side and intermediate sills. The side and intermediate sills were repaired with epoxy and new fir splices. The decking on the ends was replaced

All of the siding on the caboose was replaced with siding milled to accurately reproduce the original siding. The old roof was also removed and a new roof constructed. The roof walks were replaced and the smoke stack was repaired. The caboose was primed, painted and stenciled to the appearance it had 1953.

By the middle of August 2007 restoration was essentially complete. The restoration was completed under the direction of Karl Schaeffer with the dedicated assistance of about a dozen volunteers who contributed thousands of hours of work over a year and a half period of time. Please come by the Ridgway Railroad Museum to see the results of the restoration.

D&RGW Caboose 0575 in service, ca 1940. *Ridgway Railroad Museum.*

D&RGW Caboose 0575 undergoing restoration in summer 2007. *Photo by Don Paulson.*

D&RGW Caboose 0575, April 2008. *Photo by Don Paulson.*

RGS Motor No. 1 - Original to Re-Creation
Karl Schaeffer

Elsewhere in this volume is the story of how the Motors, later known as the Galloping Geese, helped keep the RGS operating for 20 years. This is the story of the prototype and the re-creation of the prototype. In early 1931 the RGS receiver Victor Miller and Superintendent Forest White were looking for ways to save money and had Ed Randow start on an automotive based replacement for passenger trains. The RGS then hired Jack Odenbaugh of Dolores as their Master Motor Mechanic. Jack arranged to purchase a 1925 Buick Master Six Touring car (model 1925-46) from some folks in Dolores for $50. It was brought to Ridgway about May 1, 1931 and work was begun. The RGS ended up spending about $800 to rebuild the engine and convert it to the prototype of the famous RGS Motors.

One notable feature was the use of the Buick rear axle modified for narrow gauge and with steel tires on wooden wheels. Motor No. 1 went into service on the passenger train schedule between Telluride and Dolores on June 17th on a daily round trip. It operated successfully in this service until the RGS was closed down by snow on February 8, 1932. It is claimed that it paid back its construction costs with avoided labor costs alone in about 3 weeks. No wonder they built 6 more! No. 1 operated a total of 36,250 miles over a period of 710 days before it was scrapped and parts were used to build No. 6 and to maintain No. 2. It last operated on May 14, 1933 when it had a "broken bearing" east bound at Priest Gulch at MP 77.7. It was not rebuilt because it was functionally obsolete after the much larger Motors were built. Most of this history came from dispatcher Train Sheets at the Colorado Railroad Museum.

I am a retired railroader (23 years with the Denver & Rio Grande Western, Southern Pacific, and Union Pacific). After retirement, I moved back to my favorite place in the mountains of Colorado, a few miles west of Ridgway. By chance, some folks were trying to start a local railroad museum. I got intensely involved, and decided that the best contribution I could make would be to re-create the missing Motor No. 1. My plan was to make it fully functional and capable of being regularly operated on the remaining narrow gauge railroads in Colorado.

After studying the history and photos, I started a search on the Internet for an appropriate Buick. I found a 1926-47 in Dillon, Montana. It was last operated in 1946 and was fairly complete. I paid $1,500 for it and brought it back to Ridgway on October 1,1999. I made a hard push to get it stripped and the engine into the garage before first snow. During the winter of 1999 I rebuilt many components including the engine. Much of the engine was reusable, but I had to bore it and use Packard aluminum pistons. Other than this, everything under the hood is correct. After the first season of operation, I converted from the flat belt fan drive to a 1928 V belt drive. This is something the railroad folks may well have done by 1931.

During that winter, I also worked on the running gear. I was able to purchase the front wheels, with hubs. They are identical to the original, and are still in use on railroad inspection cars today. I had to make the axles, bearing blocks, and the complete front truck assembly out of standard milled steel shapes. I used the front truck (railroad term for wheels, axles, and support assembly) now under Motor No. 6 as a pattern, because I believe that it is the truck originally used under No. 1.

The railroad used the original Buick (wooden) rear wheels with a steel railroad 'tire'. It was my belief that I would never convince the operating railroads to allow me to operate with this arrangement. The best alternative was to make a solid steel replica of the wooden wheels. I started with one and one half inch steel plate and had it cut on a pantograph. I then machined and ground the spokes to the required oval shape. This took over 100 hours, but from 10 feet, they look pretty accurate. The Durango and Silverton Narrow Gauge Railroad made the 'tires' for me out of old steam engine tender wheels.

The rear axle is the Buick part narrowed by 19 inches. I had a local machine shop do this as well as lengthen the torque tube by 17 inches because my welding is not that good. I originally used the Buick rear springs, but later found them to be too weak. They had to be significantly beefed up.

By early spring 2000, I started outside on the frame. From scaling the photos, I concluded that No. 1 had an overall length of 19' 6" and a wheelbase of 137". To achieve this, I had to cut the frame off and extend it several feet. Additionally the deck framing had to be built. I do not know what the original frame extensions were made of, so I probably overbuilt this part. The gas tank is the Buick part moved to a new location (as was done on the original No. 1) with a 6-volt electric fuel pump hidden under the deck.

As it turned out, the vacuum system worked just fine and I only use the electric to prime the system.

On the body, the hood, radiator (original honeycomb), doors, headlights, windshield, and cowl are original Buick parts. You may have noticed that this is now a touring car body. I found the appropriate parts in a local salvage yard, and traded the sedan parts for touring car parts. I had to make the radiator cap, fenders, cowcatcher, running boards, cab, deck, and sander pots. The dash is correct with no steering wheel, and the sander controls added. I used the original bottom seat spring and had it upholstered with a leather-like material. Since the cab is considerably wider than the original Buick, I also had the seat widened. John Billings of Ridgway donated much of the bodywork including painting the Pullman Green and providing the nickel plating. Larry Billings did the glasswork. Austin Baer built and donated the special door hinges.

Railroads are very sensitive to reliability and effectiveness of brakes. Toward this end, I designed a way to use the existing controls to provide a fully redundant system. The service brake applies shoes against the front wheels and activates the rear external bands. The hand brake also independently operates the front brakes and the internal linings on the rear drums. Either system will stop the car as quickly as one can with steel wheels on greasy steel rails. This is one of the purposes of the sanders, which meter small amounts of fine sand onto the rail behind the lead wheels. No. 1 stops more quickly than any of the other Motors because it still has front brakes.

The new No. 1 moved under its own power on June 1, 2000. This was 69 years to the day after out-shopping of the original at Ridgway. We took it down to the Ridgway Railroad Museum on June 11, 2000 where we had enough track for me to start testing. In late July, we took No. 1 to Golden, Colorado to the Colorado Railroad Museum where we could test run Motor No. 1 on their ½ mile loop track. We had some problems, but succeeded in accumulating 50 miles over a weekend. In late August, we took it to the Durango and Silverton Narrow Gauge railroad for Railfest 2000. This involved running 536 miles over 10 days. No. 1 performed magnificently. We did not have any breakdowns and did not have to do any significant work. The railroad was delighted to have us and we were invited back to Railfest 2001.

The re-creation of Motor No. 1 is now used for education purposes and operated a few times each summer at the Ridgway Railroad Museum.

Karl Schaeffer's re-creation of Motor No. 1 at the Ridgway Railroad Museum. *Photo by Don Paulson.*

Karl Schaeffer's re-creation of Motor No. 1 at the Colorado Railroad Museum. *Photo by Jim Pettengill.*

How the Galloping Geese Saved the Rio Grande Southern
Karl Schaeffer

Victor Miller was appointed Receiver of the Rio Grande Southern (RGS) in December of 1929. The railroad, which ran from Ridgway to Durango via Dolores, was in bad financial condition and broken into two disconnected pieces by a large mudslide at Ames (south of Vance Junction). Miller appointed Forest White as Superintendent, cleared the slide and made many other changes, but it was not enough and the railroad was at risk of going under.

In 1931 the RGS was running steam passenger trains every day with an average of one passenger per day between Telluride and Dolores and a few more in other areas. These trains had a minimum of five employees and were using very old and unreliable equipment. The RGS also had a US Mail contract that was a prized source of income and required regular and reliable scheduled service.

Miller decided to try using converted automobiles, called 'Motors' by the RGS, to run on the rails and replace the daily steam passenger trains. One salaried Motorman who would receive no overtime would operate it. The railroad would still run freight trains for ore, coal, lumber, livestock, etc. White hired Jack Odenbaugh from Dolores and brought him to Ridgway. Jack, with the help of Lee Elwell and Jack Martin, built all the RGS 'Motors'. The first 'Motor' was a 1925 Buick touring car that cost $50 to buy and about $800 to convert. It went into service between Telluride and Dolores on June 17, 1931. White reported that it paid for itself in avoided labor costs in about 3 weeks!

The RGS shop immediately went to work on more and larger machines (Motors) and eventually built seven of them in Ridgway. The first two were Buicks and the rest Pierce-Arrows. The later machines could carry about six people and up to ten-tons of mail, milk cans and express freight. They were the UPS of their time and kept the RGS going for another 20 years.

On April 1, 1950, the US Postal Service cancelled the mail contract because of poor performance. As a last resort the RGS decided to go into the tourist business. They converted the freight box on 'Motors' 3, 4, 5 and 7 to all passenger versions that could now carry 30 people but no freight. This is when the railroad officially acknowledged the unofficial name of 'Galloping Goose' in an attempt to promote the tourist business.

There are many theories about the origin of the name, but they did honk, waddle and flap their wings (engine hoods opened for additional cooling). They ran excursions from Ridgway to Lizard Head Pass for $5.50 per person. They did not create enough revenue to make up for losses in other areas and the RGS ceased operations in the fall of 1951.

A re-creation of the first 'Motor' resides at the Ridgway Railroad Museum. Numbers 2, 6 & 7 are at the Colorado Railroad Museum in Golden, Colorado. No. 3 is at Knott's Berry Farm in Buena Park, California. No. 4 (see photo below), the only motor that is not currently in operating condition, is presently at the Ridgway RR Museum for a restoration. Upon completion No. 4, owned by the Telluride Volunteer Fire Department, will be returned to that community. No. 5 is in Dolores and often operates on the Durango & Silverton Railroad during Railfest.

The re-creation of Number 1 was done by Ridgway Railroad Museum President Karl Schaeffer in 2000 and is now the property of the Ridgway Railroad Museum. It was built out of the same model of Buick as the original. It is a least 98% accurate based on the only information available, which consists of seven photos and one sketch. It is fully operational and has run on the Cumbres and Toltec Scenic Railroad, the Durango and Silverton Railroad, and at the Colorado RR Museum in Golden. Motor No. 1 also runs on the demonstration track at the Ridgway Railroad Museum during special events.

Motor No. 4, 1940s. *Wolford Collection, Ridgway Railroad Museum.*

Restoration of RGS Galloping Goose No. 4
Don Paulson

The famed "Motors" (also known as "Galloping Geese" late in their careers) of the Rio Grande Southern (RGS) Railroad were conceived in 1931 by RGS receiver Victor Miller as a money-saving substitute for steam powered passenger trains. RGS mechanic Jack Odenbaugh created the Motors in Ridgway. Eventually seven Motors were built which helped the railroad survive into the early 1950s. Six of the original seven still exist and all but Motor No. 4 have been restored to operating condition. Motor No. 4 has been sitting next to the Telluride Courthouse for more than 50 years. The heavy snowfall winter 2007/2008 caused several of the roof ribs to break and it is unlikely it would have survived another winter.

"Galloping Goose" with capitals was the official RGS public name for the RGS "Motors" only after their conversion to the tourist version in the early 1950s and this name only applies to Motors 3, 4, 5 & 7. Before that time the RGS always referred to them as "Motors" in any official publications. Without capitals, "galloping goose" is a generic name applied to a wide variety of automotive/rail hybrids. The first public application of the words "Galloping Geese" to the RGS Motors was in a 1942 article by the Rocky Mountain Railroad Club in the Denver Post.

Motor No. 1 was scrapped in order to build Motor No. 6. Karl Schaeffer built a nearly exact operating replica of Motor No. 1 which is now located at the Ridgway Railroad Museum. Motor No. 2 was never converted for tourist use and hence should not be referred to as a Galloping Goose. Finally, Motor No. 6 was only used for railroad maintenance work and also should not be referred to as a Galloping Goose.

In late May 2008 the Ridgway Railroad Museum signed a formal agreement with the Telluride Volunteer Fire Dept (TVFD) to bring Galloping Goose No. 4 to Ridgway for a comprehensive non-operating restoration and an evaluation of a possible future operational restoration. The TVFD deserves a big thank you for keeping No. 4 in condition such that it is still possible to do this restoration after 55 years. When the restoration is finished in about 3 years, the plan is for it to return to Telluride. The Ridgway Railroad Museum will do the work and the TVFD will pay for the materials.

On May 29, 2008 the Telluride Goose made its first trip over Dallas Divide since 1953. Jamie Schuler, Fire Chief of the TVFD, and his crew had several things done prior to the move. A section of the fence at the Courthouse was removed, and the street was blocked off so that the lowboy tractor-trailer could back into place. The Ridgway Railroad Museum crew arrived at 9:00 am and the semi arrived from Cortez at 9:45. This is the same company that moves Galloping Goose No. 5 from Dolores when it makes public appearances on the Durango-Silverton and the Cumbres & Toltec Railroads. With the help of the Telluride Fireman, blocking was put in place and rail was spliced between the panel track on the lowboy and the rail that Motor No. 4 was resting on next to the Telluride Courthouse.

Larry Spencer, President of the Galloping Goose Historical Society of Dolores, climbed into the Wayne Bus Body cab and served as the Motorman as No. 4 began the 55-foot journey onto the trailer. Because the Motor was on rail that sloped toward the street, a winch on Ridgway Railroad Museum president Karl Schaeffer's truck slowly let out cable from behind the Motor, while the winch on the trailer helped ease the Motor onto the lowboy from the front. A hearty cheer from the Telluride "sidewalk superintendents" greeted the successful completion of this step. By 11:05 the Motor was chained down and ready for transport. A quick stop at the top of Dallas Divide at 11:50 provided an opportunity for photos (see photo). Arriving at the Museum at 12:10, the Motor was in place on its track by 12:45.

Goose No. 4 on Dallas Divide, May 2008. *Photo by Keith Koch.*

Ridgway as a Railroad Town
Keith Koch

When Otto Mears and his chief engineer Charles W. Gibbs began planning the Rio Grande Southern Railroad in the late 1880's there were important decisions to be made. At the southern end of the proposed railroad, Durango was the logical location to meet the Denver and Rio Grande Railroad. Where the northern end of RGS would tie into the D&RG might not have been as easy to determine. The RGS first considered but then rejected Dallas as its northern terminus. Dallas, named for George Dallas, US Vice-President, 1844-1849, was a tiny railroad town on the Ouray branch of the D&RG Railroad, a few miles north of what is today Ridgway (see map on page 8).

I would suggest several reasons for rejecting Dallas as the location for linking up with the D&RG. One was the limited amount of land available in the narrow valley at Dallas for building the railroad structures and rail yard. To build on the west side of the Uncompahgre River at Dallas would have required a bridge of about 500' in length. Dallas' water supply quality would have been inadequate to meet the needs of a larger community and the RGS. During Dallas' short existence it burned twice. It was more profitable for Otto Mears to purchase land for a new town site and sell lots where Ridgway now exists. The town site consisting of 490 acres was laid out in 1890, and soon lots were being sold as a way to help finance the construction of the RGS.

Railroad companies and town sites have an interesting history in western Colorado. Most town fathers realized that to be on a railroad line would be good for commerce, creating stability and growth for their community. Without a railroad a community might be doomed to wither away.

Because the D&RG knew that existing communities wanted rail service they were able to play "hardball." In the case of Ouray, the city leaders met the railroad's demands for land for a depot, and other financial considerations. The community of Animas City, just north of present day Durango, refused to meet the D&RG's requests. The railroad developed Durango and soon Animas City faded away. Dallas suffered the same fate, as Ridgway quickly became a center of commerce and railroad activity for the area.

The new town became Ridgway, in honor of Robert M. Ridgway who had been responsible for the construction of the RGS from the town site to Rico. An unusual feature is that the twelve city blocks bordered by Amelia St. on the west, Lena St. on the east, Sherman St. on the south, and Charles St. on the north, all have two alleys, one running east-west, the other north-south. This grid was designed to serve as firebreaks in the core of the community in the event of a fire.

As the rail was laid for the RGS, the structures to support the railroad were also built. The Ouray branch line of the D&RG was relocated to the west side of the Uncompahgre River and a large wooden depot was built near the Ridgway City Park along what is now Railroad Ave. The depot was a shared arrangement between the RGS and the D&RG. The depot was moved east across Railroad Ave and turned 90 degrees after the RGS was abandoned in the 1950s. As of 2009 it is a private residence. At Ridgway a five-stall roundhouse was constructed with a 50' turntable for turning engines.

Engine facilities were a critical part of railroad operations, as steam engines are high maintenance pieces of equipment. Ridgway, during its railroad era, had two different roundhouses at two different locations. The second roundhouse was built to replace the original roundhouse that had burned down February 12, 1906. Roundhouse fires are not uncommon. This second roundhouse was located behind the present day Mountain Market and the Ridgway Hardware store. This location was chosen because it provided much better fire protection for the roundhouse. Nothing remains to indicate that this large structure existed into the 1950s.

While there are lots of information and photos of the second Ridgway roundhouse, that is not the case of the original structure. The site is currently on private property, and with the permission of the owner, five members of the Museum visited the site. The Museum has an excellent aerial photo of the site taken by Museum member Gary Woods from his hot air balloon. The variations in vegetation clearly show the outlines of some of the features.

We were able to take measurements at the site. The turntable pit suggests a 50-foot turntable. We suspect the metal turntable was moved to the second site after the 1906 fire. From the center of the turntable to the doors of the roundhouse was just over 100 feet. The roundhouse had five stalls, and each stall had an inspection pit. The center stall also had a drop pit that allowed the removal of two engine driver wheels and the axle for servicing. There are enough foundation stones that supported posts to estimate the over all size of the roundhouse. From front to back the engine house measured 69 feet. We hope that our field measurements will help match the first roundhouse to an existing set of either D&RG or RGS roundhouse plans. Ridgway is again a growing community and the site may be developed in the future.

Ridgway Roundhouse Crew, 1914. *Wolford Collection, Ridgway Railroad Museum.*

Ridgway Street Names
Don Paulson

Ridgway, Colorado exists today because of Otto Mears, builder and first president of the Rio Grande Southern Railroad (RGS). Mears had originally intended to make the town of Dallas, near the confluence of Dallas Creek and the Uncompahgre River, the terminus of his railroad. However, his engineers talked him into locating the town 2.5 miles further south due to the availability of good water, more open space and a less difficult crossing of the Uncompahgre River. The residents of Dallas soon began to move their businesses to Ridgway and Dallas quickly disappeared.

Ridgway is named for Robert M. Ridgway who was superintendent of the Rio Grande Southern Construction Company that built the northern half of the RGS for Mears. The Rio Grande Southern ran from Ridgway to Durango via Telluride, Rico and Dolores. On May 22, 1890 D. C. Hartwell, Frederick Walsen, and Charles Nix, following Mears' plan, signed the articles of incorporation for the town of Ridgway. George Hurlburt made the first town survey map dated June 6, 1890. The present street names in Ridgway (see figure on page 40) date from the original Hurlburt survey. Mears sold lots in the new 490 acre town to help pay for the construction costs of the new railroad.

The obvious question is, "who are these men and women commemorated in the names of Ridgway's streets?" Mears did not leave behind information about this question and so we are left to speculate. However, most of them are easily explained with only one or two in question. The east/west streets are all named for men. The most obvious is Otto Street named for RGS president Otto Mears. Frederick Street is named for Fred Walsen who was a partner with Mears in many of his toll roads throughout the San Juan Mountains. Walsenburg, Colorado is also named for Fred Walsen. However, Robb Magley of the *Ridgway Sun* proposes that Frederick Street is actually named after Frederick Walsen Jr. who was involved in Silverton mining ventures and always went by Frederick while Frederick Sr. always went by Fred.

Charles Street is named for Charles Nix, a Chicago financier who owned and operated many hotels in the Midwest and was later the owner of the Beaumont Hotel in Ouray. Clinton Street is named for Dewitt Clinton Hartwell who developed Ouray's first electrical power system and was a major investor in the Beaumont Hotel.

One might be tempted to propose that Sherman Street is named for the Civil War general William Tecumseh Sherman. However, a more likely candidate is William A. Sherman, a mining speculator and local judge who signed the Ridgway incorporation papers. Hyde Street is named for Richard and Arthur Hyde, brothers who sold Fred Walsen most of the land for the Ridgway townsite. That leaves Moffat Street, which is certainly named for David Moffat who was president of the Denver and Rio Grande Railroad when the town of Ridgway was founded.

All of the north/south Streets are named for women. Mary Street is named for Mary Mears, Otto's wife, while Cora Street and Laura Street are named for Mears' two daughters. Elizabeth Street, Charlotte Street, and Amelia Street are named for the wives of Charles Nix, D. C. Hartwell, and Fred Walsen, respectively. That leaves only Lena Street unaccounted for. An extensive search of the names of wives and daughters of other Mears acquaintances did not yield anyone named Lena. However, my best guess is that Lena Street is named for Lena Stoiber, owner of the famous Silver Lake Mine and Mill just east of Silverton. Mears built an extension of the Silverton Railroad to the Silver Lake Mill in 1893. A later article in this book discusses the famous Mears gold and silver passes issued for the RGS and Silverton Railroads. In 1890, the year of incorporation of Ridgway, Lena Stoiber was one of only two people to receive gold Silverton Railroad lockets.

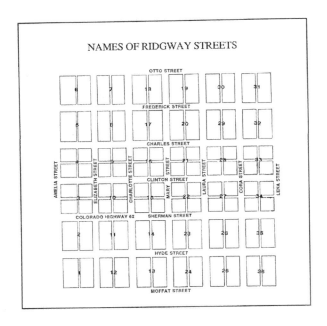

Ridgway Street Map. *Ridgway Area Chamber of Commerce.*

The Legacy of Robert M. Ridgway
Bonnie Koch

Robert Matthew Ridgway is the man for whom Ridgway, Colorado was named. He is revered as the master overseer of the laying of Rio Grande Southern track from Ridgway to Rico. We knew a lot about the positions he held in a variety of railroads, but until his great-granddaughter Sarah (Sally) Loufek visited the Ridgway Railroad Museum in 2003 and subsequently sent family information to now Museum president, Karl Schaeffer, we were missing pieces of the Robert M. Ridgway story and his dynamic legacy that would influence railroad development throughout the west.

Robert Ridgway was born on September 13, 1835 to John and Mahala Weiss Ridgway in Warren County, New Jersey. He married Sarah Jacob Schimmel in 1858 in Philadelphia. They had seven children who lived to adulthood, 4 sons and 3 daughters.

Robert's railroad experience began at the lowest level. He was only 16 when he went to work as a teamster for the Delaware, Lackawanna and Western Railroad. By the age of 21 he had worked himself up to the section gang laying track and putting in sidings, followed by the position of section foreman. During the Civil War he served as the foreman of the Construction Corps of Co. C. Second Division of the U.S. Military Railroad. A biography of his son, Amos, says Robert's service was under General William T. Sherman whose single-track railroad extended 473 miles from Atlanta to its main supply base in Louisville.

Shortly after the war ended, Robert moved to Lawrence, Kansas where he served as roadmaster for the Kansas Pacific Railroad in charge of track, bridges and buildings, his first involvement in the transcontinental railroad movement. By 1878 he held the same position for the Missouri, Kansas & Texas Railroad. In 1881, he moved to Denver, Colorado and started work for the Denver and Rio Grande Railroad serving as General Roadmaster. Two years later he was appointed Operating Superintendent of the 2nd and 3rd Divisions out of Salida. In 1890 he went to work for Otto Mears' Rio Grande Southern Railroad, as Superintendent of Construction of the 1st Division, which was Ridgway to Rico. A year later a town that would bear his name was plotted to serve as the northern connection between the RGS and the Denver Rio Grande Railroads. Robert worked for the RGS through March of 1892 when he returned to the D&RG Salida operations. After retiring in 1903, Ridgway went "home" to Kansas where he explored new endeavors. At the time of his death, Ridgway was president of the Lawrence Natural Gas Company. Shortly after celebrating his golden wedding anniversary, he died in Lawrence of a cerebral hemorrhage on June 28, 1908.

It is through articles written about him that we discover the essence of Robert Ridgway. An article published in *The Engineers' Bulletin* in 1926 identifies him by the nickname "Old Tige" Ridgway and says he had "attained an enviable reputation for ability among western railroad men." An obituary published in the Lawrence, Kansas *Journal* says, "He was a man whom people liked to meet and whom they liked even better after they met him. He had a happy disposition, and as is always the ease with a man who has a smile and a good word for everyone, he had an extremely large circle of friends. His success in business gave him a firm footing with men of the world."

An undated article from a Salida, Colorado newspaper covered a presentation of $500 in gold made to Ridgway in recognition of his employment in the Denver and Rio Grande Railroad. The group of five presenters included T.J. Guinn, roadmaster and train dispatcher for the RGS and A.W. Jones, ex-master mechanic of the Rio Grande shops in Salida. In presenting the gift, Rev. J.W. Ohl said, "It is not with the tongue of flattery that I thus address you, but in behalf of these and many others of your boys, men whom you have known these many years, who are not afraid to say things of you that you have justly merited. I count it one of the happiest experiences of my life to have been intimately associated with you, and in saying this I voice the sentiment of all present, and hundreds of others who have worked side by side with you."

He added, "And we here are conscious of the greatness of your worth as our friend and leader, and rejoice in having known and loved you." The article says that Ridgway "exhibited much feeling" upon hearing these words and receiving the gift.

Other reminiscences weren't quite as flattering. Josie Crum's *The Rio Grande Southern Railroad* contains a personal account told by James Deti. Deti later became a section foreman, but his remembrances were from the time he was only 13 and working as a water boy and general "gopher" on the Rio Grande Southern. He recalls, "Ridgway was a powerful man and had a bad temper. Once some section men were trying to pull a spike that was holding two pieces of timber together and he thought they were too slow. He walked up, grabbed an axe, pushed everybody back, hit that spike and broke it square in two".

Deti also claimed that Ridgway laid inferior roadbed to speed up the process of completing his section of RGS track (Ridgway to Rico). It is hard to know if these claims were real or the thoughts of a 13 year-old boy. They may also have been influenced by the fact that in Deti's own words there was ill will between ethnic work gangs, which may have been also directed toward supervisors.

In correspondence with Karl Schaeffer, Sally Loufek wrote, "Although my mother, who was so extremely proud to be a Ridgway resident and who passed away in 1987, did compile most of the information I now have and although as a child I would listen to many railroad tales when my mother, brother and I would travel via the Union Pacific from Lawrence, Kansas to Denver to visit my grandmother, Harriett and great uncles Harry and Arthur, it was not until we stopped at your [Ridgway Railroad] Museum that I became so engrossed. 'Twas you who inspired me. Until we talked I really had no idea of my great grandfather's status."

In actuality, it is Sally who we thank. She has given us the gift of seeing the real Robert Ridgway, a man who not only loved the sounds and sights of the "iron horse" as it steamed down the track, but inspired another generation to love it as well.

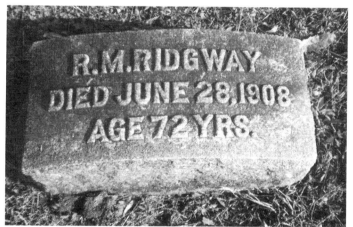 

Oak Hill Cemetery, Lawrence, Kansas. *Photos by Sarah Loufek.*

Rio Grande Southern Locomotives
Keith Koch

The men who maintained the steam engines of the Rio Grande Southern (RGS) were constantly struggling to keep the locomotives in service. It is estimated that for every hour in service the engines required an hour in the shop. A little like when one first owned a snowmobile.

Because it made good business sense and the RGS was always forced to operate on a shoestring, it was a common practice to cannibalize used parts from engines that were no longer in service. Parts were used to replace damaged or worn items, as this was much more cost effective than purchasing new ones.

Between 1940 and 1943 RGS locomotives Nos. 22, 25, and 40 were retired. These engines became the source of many parts that allowed engines such as No. 20 to operate into the twilight years of the RGS. Actually this was the second No. 20 on the RGS. The first No. 20 was eight years old when it was purchased used for $4,500 from the Denver and Rio Grande Railroad (D&RG) in 1890 by Otto Mears. The 2-8-0 Baldwin had a head-on wreck with No. 2 near the Trout Lake water tank in March of 1906, and was dismantled in 1916.

The second No. 20 came to the RGS from the Florence and Cripple Creek RR along with the second No. 22 and the second No. 25 in 1916. These three 4-6-0 sister engines had been built by the Schenectady Locomotive Works in 1899 and 1900 and were purchased used by the RGS for an average price of about $3,500. The engines were all serviced in Alamosa by the D&RG at a total cost of about $4,000 before they were put into service on the RGS.

When the tender on No. 20 began to leak in the early 1940's, the quick fix was to replace it with the tender from the recently retired No. 25. A fresh paint job, new lettering, and No. 20 looked almost new (see photo on page 46). On September 31, 1943 No. 20 was helping No. 40 upgrade near Cima. Poor track work caused No. 40 to flip over taking No. 20 with her, killing fireman Joe Wilmer. The damaged No. 20 received the wooden cab from No. 25. A "new" smoke stack and air pump came from No. 22. These replacement parts are visible in photos of the era. No. 40 was not repaired but was now another source for used parts. The RGS was careful to not dispose of any mechanical parts that might be useful in the future.

RGS No. 20, as the "Emma Sweeny," starred in the 1950 Hollywood motion picture *Ticket to Tomahawk*. It was fitted with a wooden pilot (cow catcher), an oil-burning headlamp, and a false smoke stack. As if a garish paint job with a clipper ship on the tender was not enough, RGS caboose No. 0409 was lettered for the Tomahawk & Western, "Route of the Bloody Basin Cannonball." While most of the filming took place on the Silverton Branch of the D&RGW, one scene was shot on the Lightner Creek trestle on the RGS just west of Durango. The clipper ship remained on the tender for some years after the filming.

For another example of the "make do" nature of the RGS, 2-8-2 "Mudhen" No. 455 was given a new cab after a major disaster on Dallas Divide in 1943. The unusual cab was a sectioned standard gauge engine cab that was cut down to fit No. 455 (see photo on page 46).

When the RGS was abandoned, No. 20 was purchased by The Rocky Mountain Railroad Club and is currently in Pennsylvania being restored for the Colorado Railroad Museum in Golden. In addition three other RGS engines survive: No. 41 is at Knott's Berry Farm, an amusement park in Buena Park, California; No. 42 is displayed in Durango in the Durango & Silverton Railroad roundhouse; No. 74 was removed from a Boulder, Colorado park and evaluated for potential use by the Colorado Historical Society on the Georgetown Loop RR but was returned to a Boulder when it was determined the engine had a cracked frame.

As our friends at the Durango Historical Railroad Society (DHRS) discovered with D&RGW 2-8-0 No. 315, the railroads had wrung almost all of the useful life out of their engines prior to retiring them. The DHRS has recently completed a total rebuilding of No. 315. They found parts for No. 315 from D&RGW engines No. 345 and No. 317. The engine numbers stamped on the metal item identified those parts as having been salvaged from the indicated locomotives. The DHRS is currently preparing a book about No. 315. The book will have three sections: history, technology, and the restoration of the engine and will be available in 2010.

Rio Grande Southern No. 20 at Ridgway. *Ouray County Historical Society.*

Rio Grande Southern No. 455 on Dallas Divide. *Wolford Collection, Ridgway Railroad Museum.*

The Story of RGS Coach 254
Rod Holloway and Keith Koch

Rio Grande Southern (RGS) Coach No. 254 was built for The Denver and Rio Grande (D&RG) by Jackson and Sharp in 1880. It was sold to the RGS in December of 1890 for $2,135.00. The following telegrams from the Ridgway Railroad Museum's archives deal with a serious wreck on the RGS at Porter just west of Durango.

At 9:44 am on December 28, 1895 the following telegraph was sent to W.D. Lee, Superintendent of the Rio Grande Southern Railroad:

" I consider myself to blame for accident at Porter and will respectfully tender you my resignation. A. Beers, Condr."

The reason for conductor Beers resignation became apparent by 12:10 PM when the following message was sent to W.D. Lee:

"Coach 254 sits on top of eng. 5 with sand box of eng. in doorway - one truck of coach badly broken and coach end and sides destroyed to transom - coach 202 trucks stripped from coach but trucks not badly damaged - Bage car 152 is loaded half on box car 1697 – think we can have track clear in from 3 to 4 hours and have bage 129 and coach 326 here for transfer - will advise you later how bad eng 5 is when we get coach separated from the front of eng - we may have to take coach and eng to Durango as they are. C.F.W."

It is interesting to note the following message sent at 12:55 PM to W.D. Lee.

"Mrs. Hannah B. Thompson of Dolores severely shocked - do not think there will be any claim as she is only scared - have release from balance of passengers. Reinard"

In 1896 the D&RG shops built a new coach, the second No. 260 for the RGS using the trucks from the wrecked Coach No. 254. In this era RGS coaches were painted a Tuscan Red followed by a final coat of varnish, hence the nickname "varnish" to describe coaches. By 1918 RGS coaches were being painted Pullman Green. RGS Coach No. 260 was used until the end of operations. In 1962 it was moved to the Colorado Railroad Museum in Golden, CO.

Former D&RG engine No. 245 the "Frying Pan" a 2-8-0 was built by Baldwin in 1881. It was purchased May 12, 1891 by the RGS for $4,500.00 and re-numbered RGS No. 5. It survived the Porter wreck and was in service on the RGS until 1903.

The wrecked coach No. 254 was moved to Vance Junction (near Telluride) on the RGS where it served as a depot and telegraph agency. When the RGS was abandoned Bob Shank rescued Coach No. 254 and added it to his growing collection of RGS rolling stock north of Durango. About 1984 Bob sold the coach, RGS Railroad Post Office cars No. 60 and No. 150, Geese No. 6 and No. 7, D&RGW cabooses No. 0524 and No. 0588, along with D&RGW diesel switcher No. 50 to the Colorado Railroad Museum. The Colorado Railroad Museum stabilized the coach and gave it a coat of Tuscan Red paint.

In 2000 the Colorado Railroad Museum offered RGS Coach No. 254 to a then little known organization called the Ridgway Railroad Museum. Wisely the Museum decided the coach was beyond its financial resources and labor skills.

In 2006 Don Shank did some trading with the Colorado Railroad Museum and re-acquired RGS Coach No. 254. It was transported by a flatbed truck to Monte Visa, Colorado where Don Shank would "like to bring her back" as a static display (see photo below). An excellent history of Vance Junction along with several photos of RGS Coach No. 254 can be found in *The RGS Story,* Volume III.

RGS Coach No. 254 in Monte Vista, Colorado in 2006. *Photo by Rod Holloway.*

Snow Fighting on the Rio Grande Southern Railroad
Keith Koch

"They should always be clothed for going out in bad weather, and be prepared to remain out, no matter how severe or stormy it may be." Thus read instructions to railroad men in the 1907 Denver and Rio Grande Circular No. 15.

Operating the Rio Grande Southern (RGS) Railroad in the winter was no easy task. Ice, snow, drifting snow, snow slides and freezing cold all were hazards faced by the employees of the RGS. On March 8, 1912 four members of a section crew lost their lives in a snow slide near Ames. The frontline railroad snow fighters were these section men armed with their picks and shovels. The railroad had an obligation to move freight, passengers and the US Mail. The men and their snow fighting equipment insured that regardless of weather conditions the railroad continued to operate in the rugged San Juan Mountains of southwestern Colorado.

As is the case today, the higher the elevation the deeper is the snow. Three of the highest points on the RGS were Dallas Divide, Lizard Head Pass and Cima Hill (see map on page 10). At Lizard Head Pass the RGS constructed a 1,549-foot long snow shed over the mainline and turning wye in an attempt to fight Mother Nature. It was the only snow shed on the RGS.

The RGS used a variety of equipment to remove snow from its track work. In the winter, engines and the Motors (later called Galloping Geese) were fitted with snowplows. A device called a drag flanger, patented in 1885 by the D&RG, was pulled behind a locomotive to clear the flange ways of ice and snow on the track work. Without clearing the inside portion of the rail for the flanges on the railroad equipment, derailments would occur. Originally the RGS had three of these devices.

In 1913 RGS employee Andy Rasmussen designed and built a "go devil," which combined a drag flanger with an engine wedge snowplow. This homemade piece of equipment was built in the Ridgway Roundhouse (near the current hardware store), and was lettered as RGS Plow Flanger No. 2. In less than a year Plow Flanger No. 3 was also built at Ridgway. Both plow flangers frequently derailed while plowing snow, with No. 3 having a final accident in the 1930's. Plow Flanger No. 2 survived until the end of the RGS in 1951 (see photo below). The plow flanger is an example of how resourceful the men who worked for the railroads were.

Otto Mears, the builder of the RGS in 1891, purchased two new rotary snow plows for the railroad. At the time a used narrow gauge engine could be purchased for $4,500. Mears paid $16,018 for each rotary. Rotary No. 1 was used only one year, whereas Rotary No. 2 lasted until 1949. Rotary No. 2's fate was sealed when its boiler exploded at Vance Junction.

These huge rotaries are like a giant snow blower, with blades over 9-feet in diameter. In the early days as many as five 2-8-0 RGS engines would push the rotary up 4% grades at a top speed of four mph. When working, the rotary boiler would consume large amounts of both water and coal. Because that was the case, rotaries were fitted with two tenders.

Some winters were worse than others. Prime winters on the RGS were 1899, 1909, 1913, 1916, 1932, 1944 and 1949. In March of 1912 various segments of the RGS were closed for nineteen days due to snow. It was a constant battle of man and machine vs. the harsh Colorado winters, with Mother Nature sometimes coming out on top.

Plow Flanger 2 derailed on Lizard Head Pass. *Heflin Collection, Ridgway Railroad Museum.*

Rotary Snow Plows on the Narrow Gauge
Keith Koch

Rotary snowplows were an important part of snow fighting in the San Juan Mountains on both the Denver and Rio Grande Western (D&RGW) narrow gauge system and the Rio Grande Southern (RGS) Railroad.

The rotaries were similar to today's snow blowers that dig into the snow with blades and then shoot the snow either to the left or the right. They work fine as long as there are not rocks or timber in the path of the machine that would damage the blades. The rotaries were most effective in open areas where the snow on the right-of-way was not part of a snow slide that had brought down rocks and timber.

Locomotive manufacturers built rotaries, as a major component was the steam boiler that powered the large blades. The Cooke Locomotive Works of Patterson, New Jersey was a major manufacturer of rotaries. The most successful design was patented by the Lesley brothers of Canada, who contracted out the manufacturing of the their rotaries. There were no special designs for the rotaries that operated on the narrow gauge. A standard gauge rotary was merely fitted with narrow gauge trucks.

In the early 1890's Otto Mears purchased two new rotaries for the RGS. These were numbered 1 and 2. Number 1 was used for just one winter and later was sold as surplus equipment. At the time Otto paid about $16,000 each for the rotaries. In the 1890's a used narrow gauge 2-8-0 (C-16) locomotive could be purchased for $4,500. RGS Rotary No. 2 remained in service until its boiler exploded at Vance Junction in February of 1949.

There are written accounts of RGS No. 2 being used to clear snow on the D&RGW San Juan Extension east of Chama, New Mexico. Rotary No. 2 collapsed RGS bridge 89A during the winter of 1914. The Rotaries were heavy pieces of equipment and were a poor way of testing the safety of bridges and trestles. Because of their weight and not being self-propelled, it was necessary to push the rotaries with locomotives. Often as many as five 2-8-0 locomotives were used to push RGS Rotary No. 2 up grade (see photo on page 53 for rotary No. 2 in service).

The D&RGW had four rotaries on its narrow gauge system. Rather than numbering its rotaries they used letters: OM, ON, OO, and OY. The D&RGW used the letter "O" or the numeral "0" as the first identifying mark on its non-revenue rolling stock. Caboose 0575 and water service car 04914 at the Ridgway Railroad Museum are examples of this system. The D&RGW line between Antonio, Colorado and Chama, New Mexico was almost ideal for rotary operation. On the other hand, the line between Durango and Silverton was ill suited for rotaries because of the slides. The alternative method in the Animas Canyon was the use of a ditcher and/or hand shoveling.

Each of these D&RGW rotaries has an interesting history. OM was based in Chama for use on western side of Cumbres Pass (see photo on page 53). OY was based in Alamosa for use on the eastern side of Cumbres. OY, which was purchased in 1923, was the largest of the D&RGW rotaries, weighing 140,000 pounds. Both these rotaries are now displayed in Chama, NM and are owned by the Cumbres and Toltec Scenic Railroad.

Rotary OO was purchased used in 1920 for $17,000 from the Colorado Fuel and Iron Company. The CF&I had used the rotary on its Crystal River Railroads. Because one of these roads was standard gauge, while the other was narrow gauge, the CF&I rotary had two sets of trucks. When purchased by the D&RGW rotary OO was assigned to Gunnison for use on the Crested Butte, Floresta, and Anthracite Branches north of Gunnison. Rotary OO was the smallest of the D&RGW rotaries at 80,000 pounds. Unlike rotaries OM and OY, OO operated without outfit cars (kitchen, bunk, etc.) and was tied up each night at Crested Butte or Gunnison. It was retired in 1955 and scrapped at Gunnison.

Rotary ON, which was purchased in 1889 along with OM, was based in Salida for use on Marshall Pass and the Monarch Branch. In 1942 ON was shipped to the White Pass and Yukon Railroad for service during WWII. On the WP&Y it became their Rotary No. 3. It was taken out of service in 1947, and was scrapped in 1968 at Skagway.

On March 18, 1918 as a D&RGW passenger train approached Chipeta Falls it was struck by an avalanche sending the baggage and mail cars into the Gunnison River. By the time the snow was done sliding the train was blocked both front and rear. In an attempt to rescue the passengers the railroad ordered out rotary ON. A rotary had never been used west of Gunnison because of concerns about the ability of the bridges near (old) Sapinero to handle the weight of the rotary. Those worries were confirmed when rotary ON broke through a small bridge enroute to the marooned train. With the rotary out of service the railroad used a wedge plow to reach the accident site. Among the nearly fifty passengers there were two fatalities.

Engineer Lewis Lathrop was quoted as saying "Anyone who ventured into the Black Canyon that year will never forget the experience. The thaw had caused the walls of the canyon to vomit hundreds of snow slides . . . passengers and crew were stalled there, listening to the constant thunder of running slides, not knowing when one would smash into their outfit."

D&RGW Rotary OM in Alamosa, CO, 1979. *Photo by Don Paulson.*

RGS Rotary No. 2 on Lizard Head Pass. *Wolford Collection, Ridgway Railroad Museum.*

The RGS Through Telegrams
Bonnie Koch

Among the valuable artifacts belonging to the Ridgway Railroad Museum are two boxes containing early twentieth century telegrams sent by Rio Grande Southern employees, canceled money orders, time cards from the Ridgway shops, coal tickets, shipping orders and oil tickets. Bob Richardson, founder of the Colorado Railroad Museum, rescued these two boxes when the RGS ceased operation in Ridgway in the 1950's. The RRM is currently culling these artifacts and additional materials donated by the Colorado Railroad Museum to put together an RGS employee list.

Especially fascinating are hundreds of telegrams sent by RGS employees from June through August 1910. While many of them are the "to be expected" orders for supplies and tracking of railroad equipment, some of them offer a personal look into what life was like when the Rio Grande Southern Railroad operated.

Diverse crews routinely performed railroad maintenance. June 10th, 1910 Superintendent C.D. Wolfinger, wired E.A. Herron in Telluride, "There will be six Mexican laborers on No. 7 tonight and I have given them transportation to Vance Junction." On June 27th he wired again saying, "Mr. Lee will bring a Japanese gang out of Durango in a.m. for Fall Creek section." On August 4th, J. M. Gill sent the message, "Got no laborers at Stoney Creek – need 5 or 6 italian laborers for this place."

Employees sometimes quit without warning. A June 30th telegram from Jim Johnson, Vance Junction, said, "Please arrange to send man for coal chutes tomorrow – man here quit tonight."

Valuable employees didn't show up for work. June 4th, Wolfinger, inquired, "Is Brakemen Richardson working – if so what crew is he with – if not when did he lay off and when will he be ready for work?" He followed this up with a later telegram to a doctor in Durango. "We are advised Brakeman P. L. Richardson is sick and not able to work – wish you would kindly call and examine him and advise his condition."

Working on the railroad was dangerous. On June 22nd, Superintendent Lee wired associates in Denver, "This morning, John Kemp, Bridge Carpenter, fell off bridge 19-A a distance of about 36 feet and had his left shoulder and body badly bruised. He was taken to Telluride on special train and is being treated by Dr. Hadley."

With the innate dangers, salaries needed to include benefits. June 11th from Wolfinger, "Answering your wire 10th. H. E. Orth, Fireman has $29.36 due him in June, up to and including 10th. He will have $11.35 insurance and fifty cents hospital fee to be deducted from June wages."

Sometimes employees didn't get paid "Please advise if you can wire Agent [at] Ridgway authority to pay C. W. Halk, Engine Watchman, July pay roll No. 12, Line No. 9, and if not, have check forwarded as party has left the service and waiting here [Ridgway] for his pay." W. D. Lee

Other times municipalities the railroad serviced didn't get paid "City Treasurer says we have not paid water rent for second quarter of 1910 – bill sent you first April – How?" From E.S.G. in Telluride to Superintendent Wolfinger.

Weather was a continuous challenge for the RGS. On July 30th, W.D. Lee wrote, "Mud slide one to three feet deep and thirty feet long at MP [Milepost] 48 1/4. No. 5 will be delayed about three hours. Am using section force and our bridge gang to clear." The weather system must have stayed in the area because 5 days later another wire said, "Very heavy storm Raymond to Dolores – mud and rock over the track just north and south MP 98 at MP 98 and half - water is running over tracks and track is washing out for about 25 feet and unsafe."

We associate the early twentieth century in Ouray County with the romanticism of the distant train whistle. The reality was that daily railroad life was filled with challenges coming from both man and nature.

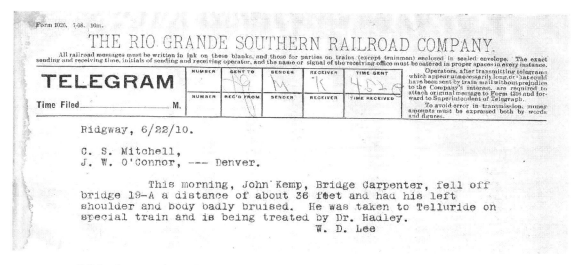

RGS telegram from Superintendent W. D. Lee. *Ridgway Railroad Museum.*

The Dark Side of Railroading
Bonnie Koch

They are over 85 years old, but when you sort through them your fingertips turn black. Some are coal tickets with lingering coal dust that were filled out by engineers on the Rio Grande Southern Railroad after having their tenders filled with coal. Others are dark lubricant smeared oil tickets from the Ridgway train yard.

Rio Grande Southern coal ticket, *Ridgway Railroad Museum.*

Archived at the Ridgway Railroad Museum are Ridgway, Vance Junction, Rico and Ute Junction coal tickets from March 1920 and oil tickets from October 1916. They are part of the materials rescued by Bob Richardson, founder of the Colorado Railroad Museum and saved until the Ridgway Railroad Museum was established. Many more have subsequently been received by the Museum.

Coal was mined near Ute Junction. It was loaded into gondolas, cars open at the top, and transported by rail to loading facilities. At Vance Junction the coal was transferred to coal chutes, but at Ridgway the gondolas were stored until the coal was used. The Ridgway roundhouse, where repairs and mechanical work were done, was located to the south of what is now Mountain Market, approximately where the present day hardware store sits. The coaling area was slightly beyond that, just east of the present day Drakes Restaurant.

Even something as simple as a coal ticket has a story. Experienced and long-time RGS engineers Ervin, McDonald, Talbert, Phillips, and Davies signed off on the coal tickets at Ridgway. According to Josie Crum in her book, *The Rio Grande Southern Railroad*, Ervin and Talbert had been part of a three-engine pile-up in 1909. Davies had ended up in the bottom of a gorge by the Butterfly Mill (MP 43) under bridge debris after an engine derailed in 1910.

Engines leaving Ridgway needed to have full tenders to make the long climb over Dallas Divide and on to Vance Junction or Rico. The tickets showed that loaded coal ranged from 1 to 5 tons with most tenders taking on 3 tons.

In Ridgway the gondola loaded with coal was placed on a raised track. The engine and tender were pulled parallel to the gondola on a slightly lower track. Coal needed to be shoveled up over the sides of the gondolas and into waiting tenders.

"Coal heavers" not only suffered from aching backs, but clenched fingers as well. Old timers told stories of fingers that cramped around the handles of shovels after hours of labor. At the end of the day, the fingers remained clenched and had to be pried open. Heavers were at the bottom of the pay scale making, in 1917, 10 cents per ton of coal shoveled! There were many jobs on the railroad that required manual labor, but this was one of the hardest, with the worst rate of pay. Yet, tons of coal were shoveled daily to provide the energy for the RGS steam engines.

Vance Junction was a major coal loading facility. Handling large amounts of tonnage created a paper problem. RGS Employees frequently ran out of coal tickets. Oil tickets were substituted with the word "oil" crossed out and the word "coal" penciled in. The gravity fed coal chutes, 7 miles southwest of Telluride, can still be seen today.

A. Nordeen signed each oil ticket at the Ridgway shop. The tickets show which engine was serviced and its destination. Generally, 1 1/4 to 1 3/4 pints of valve oil and 2 1/2 to 2 3/4 pints of car oil were required. Occasionally cotton waste was also requested. Some oil tickets were for replacement of shop supplies as on October 3rd 1916 when 16 pints of headlight oil were ordered. The coal and oil tickets also speak to the economic state of the Rio Grande Southern Railroad. Each one is imprinted with the words "Denver and Rio Grande Railroad". By 1916 the RGS was under control of the D&RG. The RGS frequently "borrowed" forms from the larger railroad.

The archived tickets may be gritty and smeared, but they provide an interesting look at the heart of the Rio Grande Southern and the day-to-day operation.

Dispatcher's Train Sheets
Bonnie Koch

Railroad buffs thrive on using trivia to revive the feel of past days when the Rio Grande Southern made its way through the canyons and over the trestles of the San Juan Mountains. Archived in the Ridgway Railroad Museum is a treasure trove of Dispatcher's Train Sheets dated between 1892 and 1951. There is one large sheet approximately 3' x 2' for each day of operation. The Dispatcher controlled the movement of trains from his office in Ridgway via telegraph. It was his job to ensure that there were no collisions along the route.

Andrew S. Meldrum completed the 1897 to 1899 sheets. Meldrum was Chief Dispatcher of the RGS after having been quickly hired on May 23, 1892 when both dispatchers quit on the same day. He would later become Acting Superintendent of the RGS from 1901 to 1902 and Superintendent from October 1903 to November 1907. In those later years he was in charge of keeping the trains operating during the mining unrest at Telluride when the section gangs and water service men were protecting bridges and track from possible attack. Miners saw the RGS negatively since it brought in the militia and carried out banished miners.

Knowing where your equipment and personnel are is a key part of the dispatcher's job. The train sheets list specific trains, numbers of the engine or engines pulling them, identification of conductors and engineers, and a list of what each train was hauling and where cars were to be distributed. A list of stations has arrival and departure times logged in for each train. Along the side of the sheet are notations on weather and temperatures.

Just as transportation arrivals and departures are a problem for today's travelers, train delays were rampant on the RGS and meticulously recorded by the Chief Dispatcher. To be expected, delays were more numerous in the winter months. June, 1898 had delays on 8 days. January, 1898 had delays on 23 days. Each entry identified what train was delayed, where the delay occurred, how many minutes were lost, and the reason for the delay.

Most delays were less than 30 minutes. Common reasons were switching, heavy trains (causing the train to move slowly), the engine not steaming up enough to provide power, mechanical repairs, and waiting at a siding for another train to pass. Something as simple as loading the cars could be a problem. Fifteen minutes were lost when train No. 6 loaded 5,000 pounds of "spuds" at Red Rock (MP 83) on December 29, 1898.

Some delays were personnel related. December 12, 1897, Train No. 12 couldn't leave the Durango Yard because they were waiting for Engineer Yates. On December 14, 1897, Train No. 11 sat at Glencoe (MP 111) for 35 minutes for the fireman to get dinner. On August 17, 1898 No. 11 was delayed 20 minutes between Dolores and Millwood because "the green fireman can't keep engine hot" and 30 minutes later between Brayton (MP 129) and Cima because of "wet rail; [and the same] fireman can't keep engine hot."

Sparks from the engine exhaust were responsible for setting bridge and brush fires. On October 6, 1898 train No. 5 was delayed at bridge 76A because" bad fires all round bridge. Bridge was afire in three places; put fire out and sent section men to watch it. No damage to bridge as yet."

Boulders, rock and mudslides, and snow were responsible for many of the major delays (see photo page 60). On May 19, 1897, train No. 7 traveling from Ridgway to Rico and pulled by Engine No. 4 ran into a major rockslide near Trout Lake. They lost an hour and 40 minutes because they had to back up about 3 miles to San Bernardo to pick up a section gang and giant powder. They then had "to shoot a couple of the largest rocks." The same train was delayed for 10 more minutes between Burns and Rico because of rocks on the track.

Sometimes a moving train couldn't avoid rocks. On February 21, 1898 train No. 7 lost 45 minutes because it "ran over a rock near Longs [MP 118, between Lizard Head and Rico] & broke train pipe & brake beam [of] rear end, car 1777 & front brake beam [of] car 1832."

Whether it is information about the work force, cargo or problems encountered, the Dispatcher's Train Sheets offer a vivid look into the daily operation of the Rio Grande Southern Railroad.

THE RIO GRANDE SOUTHERN RAILROAD COMPANY

VICTOR A. MILLER, Receiver

DISPATCHER'S TRAIN SHEET

WESTBOUND　　TIME TABLE NO. _____　*Ouray* May 26. 193_

		District No. One			
375	371	Train	372	376	Ext
m 3	mt	Engine	mt	m9	n
deCroon	McKinney	Conductor	McKinney	deCroon	Me
		Engineman			
		Engine			
		Engineman			
		Engine			
		Engineman			
515am	7pm	Time Train Crew on Duty	830am	515am	8
		Time Engine Crew on Duty			
		Time Crews Tied Up	730pm		11

		Office Designation		Miles From Durango			
	85pm 11:00 3:15	Wy	RIDGWAY	162.1	1145am 4:00 by Ry		15
			13.3 PEAK	148.8			
	10pm 1020pm	Pv	13.3 PLACERVILLE	135.5	105am 10am		11 11
1035am			11.2 VANCE JUNCT.	124.3	920am 915am	915am	10

Rio Grande Southern dispatcher's train sheet. *Ridgway Railroad Museum.*

Rio Grande Southern rock slide. *Wolford Collection, Ridgway Railroad Museum.*

Unusual Spikes on the Rio Grande Southern
Karl Schaeffer

Most people know what railroad spikes look like and they have not changed much in the last 150 years. However, in the 1890s the Rio Grande Southern (RGS) Railroad experimented with the unusual Greer spikes. They are often incorrectly called Jeffrey spikes, a reference to E. T. Jeffrey who was president of the D&RG and later the RGS President as well.

The RGS was built by Otto Mears using light, second hand rail. However, there was such heavy traffic over the line during the first full six months of operation that in 1892 Otto Mears replaced the RGS main line rail between Vance Junction and Rico with much heavier rail. Otto decided to use a new type of spike being produced in Chicago, called the Greer spike. The spikes for this 29-mile section cost $2774.91.

The new rail was 57-pound rail, which means that 3 feet of rail weighed 57 pounds. A typical length of rail is 30 feet long so it would weigh 570 pounds. Light rail (30-pound) was laid in 1890 and 1891 during initial construction of the RGS. It was soon found to be too weak.

Spikes are large nails that hold the rail down to the wooden ties. So-called 'cut' spikes that are the industry standard (see page 62) are square in cross section and have a chisel point. They are somewhat more expensive to make because they must be forged. Greer spikes (see page 62) were made by a continuous rolling process with individual spikes sheered off the rolled form. This made them considerably less expensive to produce.

Greer spikes are easy to recognize by their unique double head. The rail was laid on special tie plates designed to accept the unusual shape of the double-headed spike. They cannot be pulled with a standard spike puller and are difficult to drive with a spike maul. The biggest problem with the Greer spike is that it is thin and wears quickly from rubbing on the base of the rail, and therefore was prone to breaking off. Track maintenance people hated them and were known to throw barrels of them in the river if cut spikes were available to use instead. This is probably the only time that a vender ever got the best of Otto Mears.

Greer spikes have been found on the Silverton, Gladstone and Northerly wye at Gladstone as well as on the Colorado and Southern's Boreas Pass line. Some have also been found on mine trackage above Ouray and Telluride. Today collectors prize them. You can see original RGS Greer Spikes in the Railroad Room at the Ouray County Historical Society or at the Ridgway Railroad Museum.

Traditional "Cut" Railroad Spike

ASTM A65-01. Standard Specification for Steel Track Spikes.

Greer Patented Spike

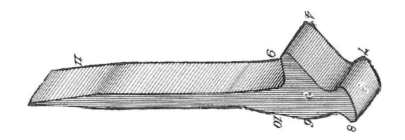

Greer Railway Spike. United States Patent 387066. July 31, 1888.

Depression Era RGS Miracle Worker: Victor Miller
Keith Koch

By 1929 the Rio Grande Southern (RGS) Railroad was bankrupt and Victor Miller, the newly appointed receiver, had many issues to resolve. For several years the Denver and Rio Grande Western (D&RGW) had been charging the RGS very high rental fees for terminals, office space, depots, and motive power. The RGS was operationally cut in two by a serious landslide at the Ames Slide south of Telluride. The D&RGW estimated a cost of $20,000 to put the line back into service. In the first of Miller's many accomplishments he was able to put the entire line back in service for $1,000.

Motive power was an area where Miller was able to save money. Before he arrived the RGS was renting engines from the D&RGW at an annual expense of $17,000 to $40,000, while the RGS was renting RGS engines No. 20 and No. 22 to the D&RGW for $12.00 per day. Miller re-opened the Ridgway Shops, returned the rented D&RGW engines, and refurbished the RGS motive power. RGS engine No. 25 was totally overhauled by the Ridgway work force for about $1,000. Two years earlier the D&RGW had charged the RGS almost $5,000 to perform a similar overhaul. By 1931 six RGS locomotives were, for the first time, able to move 1,400 stockcars during the annual fall stock rush without the use of leased engines.

In 1930 Miller was able to revise the mail contract with the U.S. Postal Service from $20,000 to $38,000 annually. Equally important, the new contract allowed the mail to be transported during daylight hours and that improved passenger service and revenue as well.

For a number of years the D&RGW was charging the RGS approximately $20,000 a year to supervise the RGS from D&RGW offices in Alamosa. Miller ended that arrangement. Without cutting the pay of employees, Miller was also able to better utilize his work force, an important step for the future of the RGS. The bankruptcy superceded the Work Rule Limits which had been enforced by the Railway Labor Act.

With the early 1930s creation of the Motors (later called Geese) a single motorman performed what a crew of five did on a stream locomotive powered train, a major labor and operating cost savings for the railroad.

Miller also addressed an unfavorable arrangement whereby the RGS paid one-third of the expense of operating the D&RGW Durango terminal. This agreement was changed to a payment based on the number of RGS engines that used the roundhouse, saving the RGS $7,500 the first year. In 1934 Miller had the RGS build its own small terminal west of Durango and saved over $7,000 the first year of its operation.

Miller might have been able to further improve the RGS operating conditions but Victor Miller's receivership ended in 1939 when he divorced his wife. Unfortunately for Miller, she was the daughter of bankruptcy Judge J. Foster Symes who asked Miller to resign and replaced him as receiver with Cass Herrington. Another factor was arguments Symes and Miller had over who would be the next RGS Superintendent.

As we look back at this era of the RGS, we tend to forget that this was the height of the Great Depression and the financial savings (dollar amounts) Victor Miller was able to institute were enormous. Railroad historians often credit Miller's leadership with enabling the RGS to survive into the 1950s.

Ridgway Roundhouse. *Wolford Collection, Ridgway Railroad Museum.*

Runaway Flatcar – the Danger of a Railroad Job
Bonnie Koch

One of the joys of working at the Ridgway Railroad Museum is the stream of visitors who come by with fascinating stories about their relatives who worked on either the Denver and Rio Grande Western or Rio Grande Southern (RGS) narrow gauge lines. These were exciting but dangerous jobs.

Fay Brewer, a friend of Museum docent and former board member Connie Schaeffer, recently provided information about her husband, RGS fireman Norton E. Brewer. Norton was employed by the RGS from 1946 to 1949. According to Fay, part of his time was spent at Rico keeping the engines warm during the winter.

Norton Brewer came from a railroading family. His grandfather, David B. Sawyer, began working for the Denver and Rio Grande (D&RG) in 1888 as a section foreman out of Salida. After also working on the D&RG Lake City Branch, he quit the railroad and moved his family to Silverton where he worked at the Silver Lake Mill. By 1926 David had returned to railroading where he worked as a section foreman out of Durango. David's son Rudolph, Norton's uncle, also worked for the D&RG.

On July 26, 1948 Norton was involved in an accident on the track near Dolores. A flat car loaded with a big boom, bridge stringers and other material was on a siding near the engine house at Rico. Two impish 12-year-olds managed to throw several switches, release the brakes, and get it traveling south on the main line. A section foreman tried to chase down the flatcar using his automobile. However, he had no luck stopping it by throwing switches to divert it onto a siding.

Traveling at about 11 1/2 miles per hour, it neared Priest's Gulch where a crew of six men were working on bridge 78-B causing the men to leap into the creek bed to save themselves. The bridge foreman gave chase in his pop-car but he was unable to get close enough to stop the flatcar.

Norton Brewer was working on a work train that had unloaded some riprap to stabilize the right of way. It had just left Stoner (MP 83) and was backing north toward the speeding flatcar. Caboose 0403 was in the front followed by several flat cars with Engine No. 41 pushing. They had been traveling about 12 miles per hour and had slowed to 4 mph to let Roadmaster Murphy off to examine a bad section of track.

Conductor McLean was leaning out the cupola window watching Roadmaster Murphy. Fireman Brewer was also watching Murphy to relay signals to Engineer Laube. Another crew member, Tucking, was on the other side of the cupola and spotted the oncoming flatcar, now moving at close to 25 mph, just as it careened around a bend and plowed into the work train.

The train airline snapped causing the brakes to halt the train. The crew yelled at each other trying to figure out who had applied the emergency brakes. The crash was strong enough to send some of the stringers on the flat car inside the caboose. If the train had been moving at its usual speed of 12 mph and had any of the crew been riding on the end platform of the caboose, as is usually the case, there would have been fatalities (see photo below). Only Brewer was injured when the force of the collision pushed his head into an engine cab window.

Norton Brewer's railroading career came to an end a year later with another injury. He broke his wrist in 1949 when a car on which he was riding while serving as a brakeman went off the track by Chicken Creek near Mancos. By the time his wrist was healed, the RGS was in decline, and he was not rehired.

Rio Grande Southern Caboose 0403, 1948 Accident. *Ridgway Railroad Museum.*

Ridgway to Placerville on the RGS
Don Paulson

Ridgway Railroad Museum members have been writing railroad history articles in the *Ouray Plaindealer* and the *Ridgway Sun* since 2005. I asked some long time readers of the *Ridgway Sun* what they would like to see in upcoming articles. They wanted to know where the railroad tracks were actually located so this article will follow the Rio Grande Southern (RGS) right-of-way as it winds its way from Ridgway over Dallas Divide to Placerville.

The RGS mainline proceeded north from the Ridgway Depot's location (at the tennis courts in the Ridgway City Park) on what is now Railroad Street. The depot was moved across the street and rotated 90 degree (see photo on page 69). Then about a block north of Otto Street the tracks turned in a northwesterly direction. The track crossed CR 5 and then CR 24A half way between Highway 62 and CR 24. Today you can clearly see the raised right-of-way in either direction from these crossings.

The tracks then followed Dallas Creek in a westerly direction one mile and crossed Dallas creek at milepost (MP) 3.2. Mile markers on the RGS start at the depot (MP 0.0) in Ridgway with Durango being MP 162. There was a lumber spur at Jay just east of the Dallas Creek crossing. Today there are two trailer houses on CR 24 at the Jay site. Several members of the Jay family worked for the RGS and one owned the Dallas Hotel at the old Dallas town site south of the current Ridgway Reservoir.

The rails then followed Pleasant Valley Creek for about five miles, crossing the creek once at MP 4.2. There were passing sidings at Hagen (MP 5.2) and Deti (MP 7.3). From Hagen to Dallas Divide the grade was the steepest on the entire railroad main line - a steady 4% grade (four feet of vertical rise for every 100 horizontal distance). At MP 8.0 the tracks crossed Pleasant Valley Creek a second time and then curved sharply to the south.

There was a section house at Pleasant Valley (MP 8.6) and a water tank about a half mile south of the Valley View passing siding (MP 9.6). Three miles further south the line crossed Hwy 62 and turned to the west to parallel Hwy 62 for the next 13 miles. The grade is clearly visible to the south of the highway for the next few miles.

Dallas Divide station was located at the crest of Dallas Divide (MP 13.3). Don't confuse these RGS MP numbers with the current Hwy 62 mile markers. The RGS called this station Peak (a misspelling of RGS dispatcher F. E. Peake's name). The facilities included a turning wye, two 26-car passing sidings, bunkhouse, coal shed, section house, section car shed, and a repair shop. In addition, there were stock pens although the stock pens there now are not the ones served by the RGS. Back in the trees is an old ranch house (restored in 2005 by Ralph Lauren) that may have provided shelter for the section men.

The downgrade from here to Brown was a steady 3%. The railroad crossed the Last Dollar Road at MP 14.6 where a small spur called Noel was used for loading hay. Leopard Creek, at MP 16.1, had a 12-car siding where hay and grain were loaded. There were several logging spurs further west at Sams (MP 17.2) and Wade (MP18.8). Sams is the location of the new turnoff for the Dave Wood Road as well as the old Ski Dallas ski area.

The RGS grade from Dallas Divide to Sams is near the creek bottom on the left. It crosses back over Hwy 62 just west of Sams and soon is fifty feet or more above the highway. You can clearly see the grade from the highway. There were several large trestles along this stretch and the concrete footings added in 1940 to Bridge 22A at Leonard, earlier called Haskel Spur, are still there. The original Dave Wood Road crossed under this trestle. The small ranch there is now called "Brown Ranch" but in the RGS era it was called the "Green Mountain Ranch."

The next station, complete with section house, bunkhouse, section car shed and a water tank, was called Brown at MP 22.2. A relocation of Hwy 62 has completely removed any traces of Brown. The RGS crossed over the highway again at Brown just west of the county road turnoff and was on the left side of the highway all the way to Placerville. There was an aerial tram for the Omega Mine at MP 25.3. The Omega was a carnotite mine from which radium, vanadium and later uranium were obtained. Unfortunately, a real estate developer removed the aerial tram several years ago; however, the upper tram house is still plainly visible several hundred feet up the hill to the east. The lower tram house became the subject for a very popular model railroad kit that lives on in many model railroads including this author's.

At the junction of Hwy 62 and Hwy 145 are the abandoned buildings of "Old Placerville" which include the Adams Hotel, a warehouse and a gas station. An RGS spur track left the mainline here and proceeded north to serve the large stock pens and further on the Texaco and Conoco Bulk-Oil Depots. These stock pens were for many years one of the principal railroad stock-loading points in all of western Colorado. The bulk-oil depots still exist but the storage tanks have been removed. Narrow gauge tank cars would be spotted on the southeast side of these buildings in order to transfer petroleum to the storage tanks. The RGS tracks left Hwy 62 at MP 26 and proceeded east along Hwy 145 into Placerville where the original depot still stands but moved one block to the east (see photo below).

The *San Juan Skyway Tour Guide*, available at the Ridgway Railroad Museum, lists many of these locations by highway mileposts which makes it easier to find them today.

Ridgway Depot, 2005. *Photo by Don Paulson.*

Placerville Depot, 2001. *Photo by Don Paulson.*

What Remains of the Rio Grande Southern Today?
Karl Schaeffer

Only a few structures and some rolling stock from the Rio Grande Southern Railroad still exist today. The Ridgway Depot is now a private home that was moved across Railroad Avenue and turned 90 degrees. About two-thirds of the former freight end of the depot was removed and the remaining third is used as a garage.

The Placerville Depot was cut into two pieces with the major section moved one block from Highway 62 and now used as a home. The smaller section is attached to the side of the general store in Placerville. The Telluride Depot was onto a new foundation, was restored and survives as the Ah Haa School of the Arts. The Dolores Depot was dismantled in the 1950s but in 1993 the Galloping Goose Historical Society completed an exact replica of this depot. There may also be some small railroad structures used as farm storage sheds that have not been identified.

Motor No. 1 was scrapped but the remaining six Motors (or Galloping Geese) survive. Nos. 2, 6, & 7 are at the Colorado Railroad Museum in Golden, Colorado. No. 3 is at Knott's Berry Farm in Buena Park, California. No. 4 (the only one that does not run) is in Ridgway for restoration as of 2009 (it will return to Telluride when finished) and No. 5 is in Dolores. The Ridgway Railroad Museum has the outhouse/coal storage building that went with the Ridgway Depot, a re-creation of Motor No. 1 and a number of smaller artifacts.

Four of the RGS locomotives survive. No. 41 is operated daily at Knott's Berry Farm. No. 42 is in the Durango and Silverton Narrow Gauge Museum in Durango. No. 20 is owned by the Colorado Railroad Museum in Golden and in Summer 2007 it was sent to Strasburg, Pennsylvania for restoration to operating condition. No. 74 has been renumbered back to Denver, Boulder and Western No. 30 and is on display in Boulder.

Four of the RGS cabooses survive. Cabooses 0400 and 0404 are at the Colorado Railroad Museum. Caboose 0402 is at Knott's Berry Farm and caboose 0409 is at Disney Land Tokyo. Passenger coaches 0252 and 0254 are in Monte Vista, Colorado and passenger coach 0256 is in Dolores. An outfit car, refrigerator car 2101, and superintendent's car "Rico" are at the Colorado Railroad Museum. Passenger coach

0257 is in use on the D&SNG. Otto Mears' private car "San Juan" (now "Edna") is restored and used at Knott's Berry Farm.

Water tanks still exist at Trout Lake, Rico, and East Mancos. The Rico tank recently received a new roof. The coal tipple survives at Vance Junction and has been restored by the US Forest Service (see photo below). In the fall of 2005 the US Forest Service also restored the last large trestle on the RGS, which is located at the south end of Trout Lake. Finally, a tender shell left over from a wreck on Keystone Hill some 100 years ago sits beside Forest Road 625 just north of the Illium Power Plant (church camp) near Telluride.

Books published about the RGS, including the twelve-volume *RGS Story*, total more than 8,000 pages. That is over 50 pages per mile! To put that in perspective, today's Burlington Northern Santa Fe (BNSF) Railroad would require almost 5000 350-page books to receive the same printed coverage per mile. The RGS, a small railroad that ran from 1891-1952 and was largely a financial failure, has developed a strong cult following among railroad enthusiasts. In the model railroad world many more people model Ridgway than live here today.

Vance Junction Coal Pockets, 2006. *Photo by Don Paulson.*

A Trip on the Silverton Railroad

The following newspaper article, from the Ouray County Historical Society archives, is reprinted verbatim from the very first issue of The Pacific Slope published in Ironton, Colorado on Saturday October 20, 1888. It is interesting to note that Otto Mears established this newspaper, as well as the Ouray Plaindealer, to provide Ouray County a Republican viewpoint in contrast to David Day's decidedly Democratic Solid Muldoon. The Pacific Slope only lasted one month but it had a significant effect on the Ouray County election results for 1888. The Republicans scored a resounding victory that is attributed to Mears' editorials.

The Silverton railroad, the screech of whose whistle can now be heard and whose train can now be seen upon the hillsides, is nothing new to the people of this vicinity, for it has been looked for, wished for and expected for some time, and the people also know something of the country through which it passes; but a brief description may not here be out of place, by one who recently went over the line.

Last summer and winter the track was completed as far as "Burro Bridge," a distance of about five miles from Silverton, and this spring construction was commenced with the usual push and energy, which the president, Mr. Mears, always displays in any scheme which he undertakes.

This road is no "wild-cat" "paper" road, but a bone fide road, built, owned and controlled by home capital, and has for its principal object, the development of the rich mines of the territory through which it passes, and also to form a "missing link" around the circle," and tourists and business people are now relieved of the hard and disagreeable stage ride between Ouray and Silverton, except for a short drive from Ironton to Ouray, which serves as a diversion to one tired of riding upon a train day and night.

About June 15 a force of about 300 men under Carlile, Price, McGavock & Co. commenced grading, and the force has been kept at from 300 to 500 till now, when the road is practically completed to the Albany mine.

To one unacquainted with railroad building, it seems almost impossible to build any sort of a road through such a country as ours, and upon leaving Sheridan and looking down upon the tops of the trees, one wonders if wonders will ever cease.

The road reaches Red Mountain and there a novelty is in store for us, for the engine is there turned and put on to the rear end of the train, and in reality the train is backed down hill still having the engine ahead. From Red Mountain the road falls rapidly, but not fast enough to keep up - or rather down - with the creek, which seems to want to hurry on to join its friends further down the valley.

The road reaches Yankee Girl mine, where by a series of switchbacks, the mine is supplied with coal and afforded transportation for its rich mineral; and by the by, the Guston also makes this the shipping point for its ores.

Passing the Little Annie the valley fairly seems to fall away from the railroad, and we now get our first view of the little town - or rather coming city of Ironton, and a more beautiful picture can hardly be imagined than is now brought to view by suddenly coming around a long, sharp curve, when Ironton and her park are now seen for the first time. The little town, nestled down among the hills so far below, and the broad level park afford such a contrast with the high mountains, which we have seen so long that they make a long-remembered picture. We see the Red mountains to the right, the Uncompahgres in front, and to the right rises a smooth but picturesque mountain that divides us from Miguel; and last, but not least, lies the town and park at our very feet. Such colors as are presented upon hillside and in early fall are not easily forgotten by one who has any appreciation of the beautiful, not even by an "old timer."

Let us now continue: Passing above the Paymaster, on to Corkscrew gulch, keeping Ironton all the time in view. Here the engine is turned, but this time on a turntable, as there is not even room for a Y as at Red Mountain. We are now fairly above Ironton, and one almost imagines be can throw a stone into her streets. We are still 550 foot above and about three miles away by the railroad, and about a quarter of a mile by trail. We now start again, but apparently away from the town.

We now again pass the Paymaster, but this time below, and when just past one can look up and see the road but a few short minutes come over, but it is at a height of 250 feet above us and looks twice as much. Soon, now, we get into the very bottom of the little narrow valley and have just room enough to turn, and in order to get room for a curve I am informed some of the heaviest rock work on the line was done. Over one ton of powder was exploded instantaneously by electricity in the large rock cut, and the debris kept a large force of men about two weeks clearing it away. We here cross Guston and Red mountain creeks on low bridges not over a hundred feet apart, and now once more get on a direct route to Ironton, with nothing of special interest except the view to the right of the country just passed over.

Silverton Railroad grade, 2005. *Photo by Don Paulson.*

The Red Mountain Depot
Don Paulson

Otto Mears built the Silverton Railroad from Silverton over Red Mountain Pass and into Ironton between the summer of 1887 and the spring of 1889 although it was essentially completed in November of 1888. In the fall of 1887 construction reached Burro Bridge, today the place where the Ophir Pass road leaves Highway 550. Mears then hired Charles W. Gibbs who had been Chief Engineer on the Colorado Midland Railroad to finish construction of the Silverton Railroad. Several major engineering problems faced Gibbs who became well known for his unorthodox engineering designs. A later article in this book discusses Gibbs' famous Corkscrew Gulch Turntable. This article describes Gibbs' second engineering marvel – the depot within a wye.

The Silverton Railroad (SRR) crested Red Mountain Pass and wound around the Knob into Red Mountain Town. The SRR right of way around the knob can be clearly seen today as you climb the last set of switchbacks on Red Mountain pass. Red Mountain Town is located in a very small mountain valley with steep sloping side hills. It is the location of the fabulously rich National Belle Mine whose head frame still sits 100 feet above the town site on the east side of the Knob. The ore from the National Belle Mine assayed at over $14,000 per ton. The Red Mountain Project has recently preserved the National Belle claim.

The railroad came into Red Mountain Town from the opposite direction that it needed to leave in order to proceed on down to Ironton. There would need to be some way to turn locomotives since the 2-8-0 engines in use did not track very well in reverse. There was no room in this small valley to locate a balloon loop and the hard rocky ground made construction of a turntable very difficult. Gibbs solved this problem by constructing a very small wye with 150-foot legs that could accommodate at most an engine and two cars. (Balloon loops, turntables and wyes are three methods available for railroads to turn equipment 180 degrees).

The wye construction was not at all straightforward since Red Mountain Creek runs through the middle of the narrow valley. Gibbs built the wye with Red Mountain Creek running through the middle of it. Because of the terrain the only place left to build a depot was in the middle of the wye. In order to accomplish this the depot had to be built on pilings with the Red Mountain Creek running under the depot. The outhouse was also placed inside the wye so patrons would not have to wait for train movements to use the facility. Switching movements must have been quite interesting in that small valley.

In 1984 Keith Koch and Mark Wilson built an Nn3 diorama depicting Red Mountain in 1890. The diorama was restored in 2005 by Don Paulson and Keith Koch and is now located in the Ouray County Museum. The photo below of this diorama shows the Red Mountain Depot inside the wye and the track arrangement at Red Mountain Town.

Red Mountain Town diorama. *Photo by Don Paulson.*

Guston on the Silverton RR
Don Paulson

The Silverton Railroad was built in 1888-89. It ran from Silverton over Red Mountain Pass and down into Ironton, a distance of only 20 miles. For a few years it was the best paying railroad per mile in the country. Among the more interesting communities along the railroad was the town of Guston.

In 1892 the Reverend William Davis was sent to the Red Mountain mining area to start a church. He first went to Red Mountain Town but was ushered out of town because the saloon and brothel owners thought a church would be bad for business. Rev. Davis followed the road about a mile north to the Guston Mine area where the mine's owner gave him a plot of land on a knoll to build a Congregational Church and a small cabin for his family. No money could be found to buy a church bell so the mining company piped compressed air to a whistle placed in the little cupola. On the day that the church was consecrated the Red Mountain Town business district burned to the ground. Rev. Davis was quoted as saying "You can't fight God and prosper." The ruins of the church and the two cabins lie flat on the ground today obscured by a heavy stand of aspen trees. The cupola still stands next to the church ruins.

Guston also had a depot on the Silverton Railroad. It was little more than a small passenger shelter on top of a loading platform but it was the only passenger shelter on Red Mountain attesting to the importance of the Guston, Robinson and Scotch Girl Mines. The shelter and platform are still there today but the shelter has been knocked over by a fallen tree.

Large mines on the Silverton Railroad usually had two railroad spurs. The Guston was no exception. The upper elevation spur was used to bring in coal and supplies. The coal could then be easily moved down into the furnaces that provided the steam power for hoists, rock drills and other uses. The lower elevation spur was used for shipping ore out. The ore could be fed by gravity through whatever milling process was used. Thus coal and ore would not have to be moved uphill. The Silverton Railroad and other San Juan narrow gauge railroads never shipped ore out in open ore cars. The valuable ore was usually shoveled into sacks and stacked in boxcars over the trucks to balance the load. Occasionally the ore was just shoveled into the boxcars, again over the trucks.

Then the boxcar was locked and a numbered seal was attached so that the shipper could easily tell if the door had been opened enroute to the smelter.

Today the upper Guston coal spur is a road that passes between the Guston Mine and the higher elevation Guston Depot. The lower spur is a long railroad grade that passes through a beautiful rock cut in order to reach the lower level of the Guston Mine buildings. There are several mine buildings left at Guston along with large yellow-colored mine dumps which can be seen from County Road 31 as it winds its way through the Red Mountain Mining District.

Guston was at its zenith in the heady silver days of the 1880s and early 1890s. The photo below shows Guston in 1900 with the church and depot marked by arrows. A boxcar is visible on the Guston Mine Coal Spur. The silver panic of 1893 and the resulting recession was a death knell for silver mining on Red Mountain as the once famous mines closed down forever. Some mining of base metals on Red Mountain continued up to the 1950s but never on the same scale as before. The Silverton Railroad never made any money after 1895 and it too was gone by 1926.

The Ouray County Historical Society and the Ridgway Railroad Museum offer hikes on the Silverton Railroad grade to the Corkscrew Gulch Turntable. Among many sites visited on these hikes are the two Guston Railroad spurs, the Guston Church and the Guston Depot.

Guston Church and Depot (arrows) in 1900, *Photo by F. L. Ransome, United States Geological Survey.*

The Silverton Railroad's Corkscrew Gulch Turntable
Don Paulson

The Silverton Railroad ran from Silverton to Albany in Ironton Park where a smelter was located. Otto Mears financed the construction of the railroad to tap the rich silver mines on the Ouray side of Red Mountain Pass. In the fall of 1887 the railroad was completed as far as Burro Bridge where the Ophir Pass Road crosses Mineral Creek below Highway 550. The next spring Mears hired Charles Gibbs as the construction engineer and he built the railroad from Burro Bridge to Albany in less than 8 months! Gibbs constructed three remarkable engineering features between Burro Bridge and Albany: the Chattanooga Loop, the station inside the wye in Red Mountain Town and the Corkscrew Gulch Turntable.

As the railroad descended Red Mountain Pass, a switchback was required at the head of Corkscrew Gulch since there was not enough room for a balloon loop or a wye (two common methods for reversing the direction of a train). However, putting in a switchback would require the 2-8-0 engines to back down or back up the grade from the switchback. This was bad for three reasons. First, these engines were prone to derail when going backwards, especially in snow. Secondly, it was dangerous to back a loaded train downhill, and finally, it was necessary to have the engine positioned at the correct end of the train when switching the various mining spurs. Gibbs' solution was to place a turntable on the mainline.

The Corkscrew Gulch Turntable is reputed to be the only turntable ever constructed on the main line of a US railroad. Gibbs described the operation of the turntable in a famous article in the *Transactions of the American Society of Civil Engineers* in September of 1890. A typical train had from three to five cars. The figure on page 80 shows the trackage at the turntable. The track grade leading onto the turntable was downhill to the turntable in both directions allowing the cars to run through the turntable by gravity after the engine was turned. So the grade coming up from Ironton actually climbed a few feet higher in altitude than the turntable so that the approach to the turntable was always downgrade.

A train coming upgrade from Albany would stop at point B, the engine would be uncoupled, run onto the turntable, turned and then run to point A. The cars would then be run through the turntable by gravity and the engine would re-couple to these cars and proceed upgrade to Silverton with the engine in front. Similarly, a train coming downgrade from Silverton would stop at point A. The engine would be uncoupled, run onto the turntable, turn and then run to point B. The cars would be allowed to run through the turntable by gravity and the engine would couple on to them and proceed downgrade to Albany with the engine in front. The entire process took about five minutes.

The ruins of the turntable on the north side of Red Mountain No. 2 can easily be visited along with several miles of right-of-way, some with ties still in place. The Ridgway Railroad Museum and the Ouray County Historical Society sponsor several guided hikes each summer and fall along the Silverton Railroad right-of-way and to the turntable site.

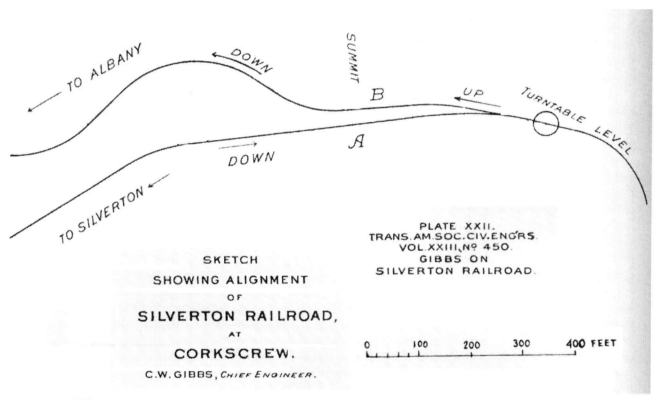

Gibbs, C.W., Transactions of the American Society of Civil Engineers, Vol. 23, No. 450, 1890.

The Mears Railroad Passes
Jim Pettengill

By the late 1880s Otto Mears was known as the "Pathfinder of the San Juans." A self-made man, he had built a network of toll roads that form the basis of today's highway system, and he was embarking on a new career: railroad magnate. He built two narrow gauge lines out of Silverton, the Silverton Northern towards Eureka (and eventually Animas Forks), and the Silverton Railroad over Red Mountain Pass to Ironton and Albany. In 1891 he built the famous Rio Grande Southern (RGS) from Ridgway through Telluride and Rico to Durango.

To promote these railroads, Mears issued complimentary passes for travel on his Silverton Railroad and RGS. Such passes were not unusual; many railroads issued them. What made Mears' passes unique was their flamboyant construction. While other railroads issued their complimentary passes made of card stock, Mears had his made of buckskin, silver and gold! These passes were issued to family members, friends, employees, and influential people in industry and politics.

The buckskin passes were issued in 1888 and granted the bearer free passage on the Silverton Railroad. They were printed with a scene depicting a steam train rounding the Chattanooga curve at the southern base of Red Mountain Pass. For 1889, Mears reasoned that a special pass from the Silver San Juan should be made of silver. They show a scene similar to that on the buckskin passes, and bear the stamped or raised signature of Otto Mears.

The 1890 passes were unique. They were smaller, in the form of a silver watch fob with blue enameled bands that read "Rainbow Route" (a name for the line coined by Mears' best friend, David Day, the editor of Ouray's *Solid Muldoon* newspaper) and "Silverton Railroad". Two gold lockets were made from the pass die, and may have been honored as passes. They were presented to Lena A. Stoiber and Rasmus Hanson, both prominent mine owners.

Mears did not issue passes in 1891, but his 1892 passes are the most famous of all. The December 31, 1891 *Ridgway Herald* announced "President Otto Mears, of the Rio Grande Southern railroad, has ordered Mr. S. Spitz, a filigree manufacturer of Santa Fe, to furnish him at once 500 annual passes over his road manufactured of filigree silver.

The pass will consist of a silver rim, about the size of an ordinary calling card, filled in with delicately frosted filigree, resting upon which, in raised letters of burnished silver, are the words, 'Rio Grande Southern Railroad Pass, 1892, Otto Mears, President.'" The passes also listed the "Silverton RR" and came with a leather case.

Records show that three gold filigree passes were produced in 1892. One was given to Mears' daughter Cora, and another to A. J. Clark, an original investor of the Silverton Railroad. The recipient of the third gold pass is not certain, but was probably either U. S. Senator H. M. Teller or David Day. Day received special treatment from Mears, and was always issued pass number one. Day's wife wrote that Mears had given him a gold pass, but that it had been stolen in Denver.

The Silver Crash of 1893 plunged the nation into a deep depression, and brought the end of the Mears passes. These mementos of Ouray County's narrow gauge history have become world famous. At least 200 existing passes have been cataloged, many in museum collections – but who knows how many others are tucked away in attics, or in safe deposit boxes? Silver passes, complete with leather cases, have sold recently on eBay for thousands of dollars! What a stir it would cause if the missing 1892 gold pass were to show up on *Antiques Roadshow.*

Mears' silver filigree and silver engraved passes. *Colorado Historical Society (ID# 20100), all rights reserved.*

The Silverton Northern Railroad's Motorcar
Keith Koch

The Silverton Northern Railroad was one of Otto Mears' three short lines that operated out of Silverton, Colorado. On August 3, 1908 the Silverton Northern took delivery of a motorcar built by the Stover Motor Car Company of Freeport, Illinois. The car was designed to carry twelve passengers and was powered by a 30-horsepower four-cylinder engine, which is not much in the way of power, the kind of horsepower you find on a large garden tractor. The photo on page 84 shows this motorcar with Otto Mears on the left and J. R. Pitcher, Otto's son-in-law and the General Manager of the Silverton Northern, to Otto's left. The back of the photo identifies the third man on the left as Mr. Stover. The women in the car are Otto's wife and daughter.

In 2007 the Ridgway Railroad Museum received a bound collection of 500 letters from the Pitcher era of the Mears' railroads. In a letter to the Stover Motor Car Co. on June 24, 1909, General Manager James Pitcher writes: *"Kindly advise us if it would be feasible to install a six cylinder engine in place of the four in the car we purchased from you about a year ago and if so what would be the cost and H.P. of the engine, with magneto, that you would furnish.*

The car, when used on grades not exceeding 3%, gives absolute satisfaction and can be run continuously without adjustment or repairs but as soon as we tackle the 6 1/2 % grade the engine overheats and the excessive speed at which is necessary to run the engine racks (sic) *the car to such an extent that frequent repairs are necessary.*

We believe that if the car were equipped with a six cylinder engine of adequate H P. it would give entire satisfaction, in which event we would be in the market for more. In quoting your price for another engine, we think it is only fair that you take into consideration the fact that the car as it stands has never operated successfully on the heavy grades for which it was designed."

The heavy grades referred to were from Eureka to Animas Forks that at one point reached 7%. Typical Colorado narrow gauge grades were in the 3% to 4% range. The suggestion of buying more Stover railcars may have been nothing more than an attempt to get a better price on a new six-cylinder engine.

When Pitcher wrote the Stover Motor Car Co. on January 22, 1910 his attitude had changed. *"Replying to yours of Dec. 12: we suggest that you recover from Mr. Stover the letters in question as we have neither the time nor the inclination to again go into the faulty design and inferior workmanship applied to the car which we purchased from you. In view of the tone of your letter, which convinces us that you have prejudged our claim, we prefer to let the matter drop.*

The mere fact that the car cost you more than the price you charged us has no bearing on the efficiency of the car and merely indicates that you did a poor stroke of business as well as building a poor apology for an automobile. If you really think the car is worth considerably more than we paid for it, we would be glad to have you find us a customer for it at considerably less than the price we paid you."

An analysis of the problems Pitcher was having with the Stover railcar might be explained in several ways. The railcar could not be tested on 7% grades in Illinois. The railcar with a 30 H.P. engine was underpowered for the grades it was attempting to climb. The engine, like any with a carburetor, was not very efficient at Animas Forks, elevation of 11,080 feet, because of a lack of oxygen. The overheating issue also is related to altitude, as water boils at a lower temperature at higher altitudes, and lower air density results in lower heat transfer, an additional cooling problem.

This rail bus history is important to narrow gauge railroading in the San Juan's, as it foreshadows the coming of the Rio Grande Southern Railroad's Motors in the 1930s, which later became the world famous "Galloping Geese."

Silverton Northern Motorcar No. 1. *Colorado Railroad Museum.*

Otto's Impossible Dream: Ouray to Ironton by Rail
Jim Pettengill

In 1883 the Red Mountain Mines were booming and Silverton and Ouray were competing for the district's business. Unfortunately for Ouray, there was no road to Red Mountain, just dangerous pack trails. Two companies had tried and failed to build a road up the Uncompahgre gorge.

Ouray turned to Otto Mears, who agreed to build and control a toll road, and on September 8 the *Red Mountain Review* reported, "That Hon. Otto Mears is the veritable 'Moses' appointed and selected of the Almighty to lead Ouray out of the 'slough of despond' cannot now be doubted. He has just completed arrangements to lay an iron rail tramway from Ouray to the Red Mountain mines. It will be operated by mule power, the loaded cars to be run down grade and managed by means of brakes, and the empty cars to be hauled back by mules. The grading on the road is almost completed, and the bed will be wide enough for a wagon road along side of the tramway." As you might expect, the tramway was not installed, possibly due to a shortage of brave (or foolish) brakemen.

Mears never gave up on his dream of connecting Ouray to the Red Mountain area by rail. Between 1887 and 1891 he built the Silverton Railroad between Silverton and Ironton and the Rio Grande Southern from Ridgway to Durango by way of Telluride and Rico. While the RGS was under construction, the forward-thinking Mears proposed an electric railroad to connect Ouray to Ironton. Ouray's first direct current electric plant was built in 1885, and subsequent developments, which included L. L. Nunn's construction of the world's first commercial alternating current station at Ames in 1890, placed electrification on everyone's minds. In 1891 Mears and his partners incorporated the Ouray and Ironton Electric Railway, Light and Power Company. An amazing route up the canyon was surveyed that paralleled the existing wagon road. It included a tunnel, a 360-degree loop near the present Camp Bird road, and averaged a seven percent grade. See page 87 for the logo accompanying the railroad survey map.

Mears' vision for the line was clear. In the March 10, 1892 *Solid Muldoon* he stated: "I think an electric motor can be operated on that line easily as there are motors manufactured which overcome heavy grades as heavy or heavier than any on that line.

My plan is to equip the line in an elegant and substantial manner and make it attractive to tourists, and it will be utilized to handle freight, too. The cost, I estimate, will be about $800,000. The system has not been decided upon yet, so I cannot say whether it will be overhead or storage battery." The February 23, 1893 *Ridgway Herald* stated that: "The road will be worked by the trolley system . . ."

Construction was to begin in 1892, but was delayed a year. Heavy snows buried the Uncompahgre canyon until late spring, and Mears decided to extend the RGS to California and directed his engineers to lay out the route.

Construction in 1893 was further delayed, and then the precarious house of cards that supported silver mining in the West fell apart. India demonetized silver in early June. Four days later the price of silver had dropped 25 percent and banks and mines closed all over Colorado. On June 17 the stock market crashed, and on August 1 Otto Mears lost control of the RGS. By the time the Sherman Silver Purchase Act was repealed in November 1893, the electric railroad was dead.

Or was it? On January 25, 1900 the *Ouray Herald* reported that Charles Nix had begun work on the Bear Creek dam on the Uncompahgre, which was to supply power for the electric railroad, the City of Ouray, and area mines. Completion was expected that year. On February 1 the *Herald* reported "The road will be laid on the Mears toll road . . . Mr. Mears said yesterday that everything was nearly ready to commence the construction of the line, but that nothing would be done until the building of the plant for the generation of power was assured."

That would be more than two years in the future. In the meantime, Mears' franchise to operate the toll road expired and citizens of the county refused to allow the road to be converted to a railroad, as they considered loss of the route to conventional travel unacceptable.

The idea revived briefly in 1905 when the *Ouray Plaindealer* reported that Mears was considering construction of a cog railway between Ouray and Silverton. It would be similar to the one that was built up Pikes Peak in 1891, and follow a new route that would not impinge on the wagon road. However, Mears was unable to arrange funding, and despite another proposal promoted by the *Plaindealer* in 1910, Otto was never able to fulfill his dream of rails up the Uncompahgre.

PRELIMINARY LOCATION OF THE
OURAY-IRONTON
Electric Railway.

IRONTON to OURAY.

OURAY COUNTY, COLO.
1892

R.L.KELLY
Engineer

GE.HOWARD.
Asst.

Logo from Survey Map. *Ouray County Historical Society.*

The Other Otto Mears
Don Paulson

Almost everyone reading this article has heard of Otto Mears, "The Pathfinder of the San Juans." He built or completed numerous toll roads in the San Juans including the road between Ouray and Silverton as well as the Camp Bird Road. He also built two railroads in Ouray County and owned four railroads in the San Juans. However, few people are aware of the other endeavors that he was involved in during the late 19th and early 20th centuries.

Otto was a back-room politician and a life-long Republican who was very influential in Colorado. In 1871 Mears started his political career in Saguache County where he served three terms as county treasurer and beginning in 1881 he served one term in the Colorado State Legislature. For over 30 years he was on the Colorado Board of Capitol Managers and managed the construction of the Colorado State Capitol building in Denver. Few Colorado governor or US Senate candidates were successful without Mears' active endorsement.

In 1888 in order to provide a Republican voice to counteract David Day's *Solid Muldoon,* which supported the Democratic Party, Mears financed two new newspapers in Ouray County, The Ironton *Pacific Slope* and the Ouray *Plaindealer*. For several years Mears reportedly wrote most of the editorials in these two newspapers. Surprisingly, Mears and Day were the best of friends throughout their careers, agreeing on most topics except politics.

In the mid-1870s Mears provided mail service to many towns in the San Juan Mountains and at one point even delivered the mail himself in the dead of winter using snowshoes and dog sleds. He owned a number of supply stores in Saguache, Del Norte, Lake City, Ouray and Silverton and a hotel in Montrose. Mears was a friend of Chief Ouray and was involved in several of the treaties with the Utes in 1870s.

In 1897 Mears accepted an offer from David Moffat, D&RG President, to move to Maryland and complete the construction of the Chesapeake Beach Railway. After completion of the railroad he moved to Washington, D.C. In 1902 he was forced to resign because of a disagreement with investors and he lost his stock in the railroad. This was unfortunate for Mears since the railroad became very profitable.

In 1902 Mears, the consummate politician, worked hard for the election of William McKinley and was rewarded by appointment as head of the committee to plan President McKinley's inaugural ball. Later that year Mears moved to New York where along with James Pitcher he invested in the Mack Brothers Motor Car Company. Mears and Pitcher became good friends and Pitcher made many visits to Mears' home in New York where he met Otto's daughter Cora. James and Cora were married in 1904.

During his time in New York Mears also turned his attention to railroading in Louisiana by attempting to build a 195-mile railroad from Monroe to New Iberia through the Louisiana swamps. This venture ended soon when he was outmaneuvered in obtaining a right of way into New Orleans but Mears was enthralled by the Louisiana culture and was even in charge of planning the 1905 Mardi Gras celebration.

In 1905 Mears was elected president and Pitcher secretary/treasurer of the Mack Brothers Motor Car Company. In 1906 Mears had a falling out with the Mack stockholders and he and Pitcher left the company. Mears brought Pitcher back to Silverton with him and Pitcher became the manager of the Silverton Northern Railroad, which also operated the Silverton Railroad. On page 90 is a photo of Mears' house in Silverton.

Otto Mears was also involved in numerous mining ventures in the Silverton area, often with James Pitcher. Mears treated his mine and mill workers very well which was extremely enlightened for the era, much in the same way as Tom Walsh. Mears had enormous success from 1907 to 1920 with his many mining operations in Arrastra Gulch located northeast of Silverton, which included the Iowa-Tiger Mine, Silver Lake Mine, Silver Lake Mill and a mill he owned with Arthur Wilfley the inventor of the Wilfley concentration table. Wilfley did considerable research on his famous table at the Mears/Wilfley Mill. Wilfley became very rich from the Wilfley table and later the Wilfley sand pump. The sand pump was invented to move the old tailings from Silver Lake down to the Mears/Wilfley Mill. You can still see the foundation of that mill on the north side of Animas River just upstream from the Silver Lake Mill located on the south side of the river.

Mears became quite wealthy from these mining ventures and in 1913 he bought the Maryland Hotel in Pasadena, California. He eventually retired to Pasadena in the early 1920s and died there in 1931. In 1926 the *Silverton Standard* raised the money to place a plaque honoring Mears at the former site of his Bear Creek Toll Booth. Otto was unable to attend the dedication ceremony in 1926 due to ill health but he did return in 1927 (see photo below). The plaque reads "In Honor of Otto Mears Pathfinder of the San Juan, Pioneer Road Builder, Built this road in 1881." The plaque was removed during a road widening project in the 1960s. In the early 1970s Joyce Jorgenson, then owner and editor of the *Ouray Plaindealer*, found it and convinced the highway department to repair it and reinstall it at Bear Creek where it can be seen today.

Otto even had a Liberty Ship named after him. During WWII any group that raised war bonds worth more than $2,000,000 could name a Liberty Ship. Over 2700 of these ships were built to transport troops and supplies to Europe. The SS Otto Mears was built in 1943 by Permanente Metals Corporation located in Richmond, California but I have not been able to find out who named the ship. In 1947 it was sold to an Italian shipping company and eventually scrapped in Singapore after catching fire in 1967.

Otto Mears' house in Silverton, 2003. *Photo by Don Paulson.*

Otto Mears and his Bear Creek Falls Plaque, 1927. *San Juan County Historical Society.*

The Ouray Depot
Tom Hillhouse

Most Ouray residents don't realize that some 80 years ago a bustling railroad yard was located at the north end of Oak Street on the site of the 4J + 1 + 1 Trailer Park. This yard was presided over by Ouray's uniquely designed 1888 Denver and Rio Grande Railroad depot. The photo on page 92 shows the depot in the mid 1940's.

Although the Ouray Depot was based on standard Rio Grande design, it featured a unique hip roof that provided for a three-room agent's quarters on the second floor above the office and waiting room. As such, it was unique to the entire D&RG system.

The Ouray depot was built by a crew of D&RG carpenters and laborers who arrived by train in July 1888, six months after the arrival of the first train. In just two months' time they had completed the building and on the morning of September 28, 1888, outgoing passengers departed from the new depot for the first time. The *Ouray Herald* characterized the depot as "one of the costliest little depots on the line of the D&RG railroad."

For the next 60 years the depot would serve as Ouray's link to the outside world. Through it would flow merchandise, supplies, food, telegraph information, and of course, ore from the many surrounding mines in the San Juan Mountains. In the early 1900s Ouray played host to as many as ten daily trains. However, the emergence of automobiles in the 1920's and the Depression of 1929 took a heavy toll, especially on passenger service, which was eliminated in 1936.

In May 1948 at the Church Ranch, two and one half miles north of Ouray, an eleven thousand volt power line owned by Western Colorado Power Company was toppled by rampaging floodwaters of the Uncompahgre River. This resulted in voltage being sent through the railroad's telegraph system up and down the line. In Ridgway the depot caught fire doing $5,000 damage to the building and the agent's personal belongings. The Rio Grande Southern Roundhouse also suffered a small blaze, although it was quickly snuffed out. In Ouray, however, the depot fire gained considerable headway before being noticed. The Ouray firefighters were hampered by low water pressure and were unable to control the blaze. The depot and all its contents, including freight and express shipments were a total loss.

For the next five years Ouray's depot and freight office was two converted boxcars. On March 21, 1953 the last train to service Ouray took ten cars, including the two converted boxcars and left Ouray ending 66 years of railroad service for the town.

The land that belonged to the D&RG was given back to the City of Ouray. For the next three years the city discussed turning the former railroad yards and depot site into a ten-acre city park. Among the plans were the planting of 100 poplar trees, the building of drives, campgrounds, and a playground for children. The city was not able to follow through with its plans and in 1957 sold the land at auction to Jack and Jacqueline Clark who built the 4J+1+1 office building on the foundation of Ouray's D&RG depot.

So as you drive along Oak Street today and see the 4J+1+1 office building, stop for a minute and think of the days gone by when this site was the center of activity and source of news for the citizens of Ouray. You can learn more about the Ouray Depot and the disastrous fire by visiting the Ouray County Museum at 420 6th Ave.

Ouray Depot, 1940, *United States Library of Congress.*

The D&RG Yard in Ouray
Don Paulson

The Denver and Rio Grande Railroad built the Ouray Branch in 1887. The track entered Ouray on what is now County Road 17. The yard extended from approximately across from the swimming pool all the way beyond the D. C. Hartwell Lumber Company, which later became the Rice Lumber Company, to the Beaumont Sampler and the power station. The track was soon cut back to the lumber company. There were also several industrial sidings just to the north of town. See the 1905 map on page 95 for most of the buildings discussed in this article.

The Wanakah Mill siding was located just south of where Corbett Creek crosses County Road 17. The concrete foundation is still sitting among the weeds to the north of the road. The long trestle here was called the Mill Trestle even after the mill no longer existed. The next siding to the south was the so-called Bachelor Switch located just to the south of the entrance to Whispering Pines. It served the Bachelor and other mines as well as local dairy farmers. There was a short siding at the American Nettie Mill now known as the Silvershield Mill. Finally, the Grand View Mill spur was located just south of the mobile home park on the west side of County Road 17. Craig Hinkson built the first of four condominium buildings on the foundation of that mill.

As the tracks came into town the first railroad structure encountered was the 50-foot turntable, which could turn a small 2-8-0 engine with only a few men pushing on each end of the turntable. The turntable was located where the small red shop building nestles into a curvature of the rocks on the west side of the road. An old dump truck currently sits at the north end of that building. Immediately to the south of the turntable was a two-stall engine house. Early postcards of the Ouray Pool clearly show the engine house directly across the river. It burned down in June of 1900 and by the end of September a two-stall engine house from Sapinero was moved to the same spot. This second engine house also burned down in 1935. There was also a short outdoor storage track to the west of the engine house.

Next to the south in quick succession came an ice house, small stock yard, the Continental Oil Company warehouse, a long set of coal chutes, a tool house and a bunk house. These were all on the east side of the tracks. The yard was three tracks wide from the turntable to the tool house where it dropped to two tracks.

The beautiful Ouray Depot was built at the foot of eighth street in 1888, six months after the railroad reached Ouray. It stood where the office of the 4-J+1+1 Mobile Home Park is now located. Before the depot was built the D&RG used two modified boxcars as a depot. The depot burned down in 1948 after a small flood washed out an 11,000-volt power pole north of Ouray that fell on the D&RG telegraph line. The power surge started fires in the Ouray and Ridgway depots and in the Rio Grande Southern Roundhouse in Ridgway. Since the agent lived in the Ridgway Depot he was able to put out the depot fire and RGS crews quickly put out the roundhouse fire. By the time the fire was discovered at Ouray the depot was engulfed in flames. Once again a boxcar served as the depot from 1948 until the line was abandoned in 1953.

Just north of the depot a short spur crossed the Uncompahgre River to serve the Munn Brothers Sampler at the foot of Sixth Street. The railroad main line also served a beer and ice company and the Kramer and Bushkick Warehouse. The main line crossed the Uncompahgre at Fourth Street to serve The D. C. Hartwell Lumber Company, the Reed and Reynolds Warehouse and the Ouray Electric Light Company. Originally, it also proceeded a bit further south to the Beaumont Sampler. The last 900 feet of track from fifth street south was removed in 1909. The D&RG Ouray branch between Ouray and Ridgway was abandoned and the tracks removed in 1953.

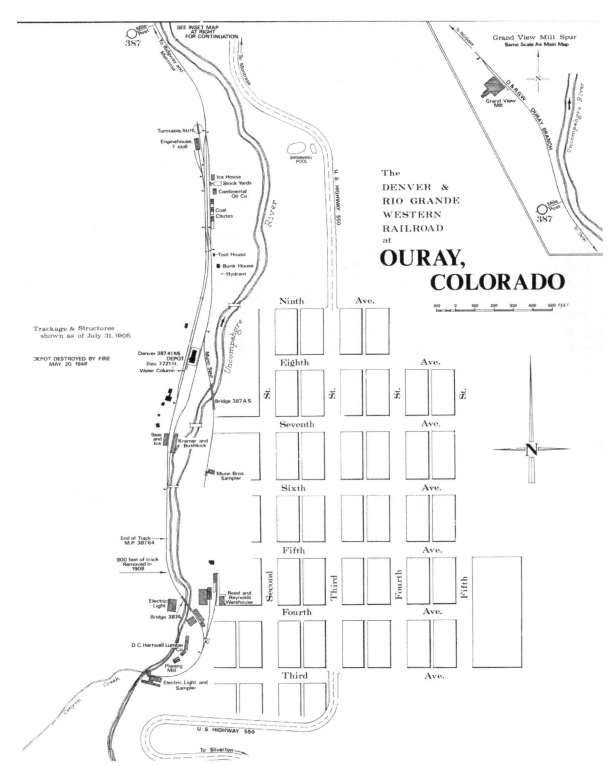

Map of D&RGW tracks in Ouray as of 1905. *Colorado Railroad Museum.*

Two Denver and Rio Grande Railroad Lines Through Ridgway
Karl Schaeffer and Don Paulson

In 1887 the Montrose to Ouray line of the Denver and Rio Grande (D&RG) Railroad passed through the town of Dallas just north of what is now County Road 24. In the late 1880s the town of Dallas was an active community, but Ridgway did not yet exist. Dallas was located in the flat area east of the Uncompahgre River just to the south of the Ridgway Reservoir. Dallas was founded in 1880 and named after the former Vice President (1845-1849) of the United States, George M. Dallas. It was a stagecoach stop on the toll road that linked Montrose with Ouray. Dave Wood's freight line served Dallas, Ouray and Telluride.

From November 1887 until 1890 the D&RG track from Montrose south to Ouray passed through the east side of what would later become Ridgway on what is now US 550. The railroad crossed over to the other side of the valley just south of the Orvis Hot Springs on what would become County Road 3. The D&RG line stayed on the east side of the Uncompahgre River down to a point just north of the current County Road 3/3A bridge over the river. It then crossed the river and followed what are now CR 23 and CR 17 on into Ouray. This bypassed Dave Day's Ramona town site as described in another chapter in this book.

In 1890, the D&RG built a wooden Howe Truss bridge across the Uncompahgre River at the north end of Ridgway. This wooden bridge was later replaced with the iron structure (moved from the D&RG Arkansas River line) that is now part of the bike path (see photo on page 97). When you are on the bike path look at the northwest corner of the bridge where you can plainly see "Arkansas River" stamped on the front of the iron truss. The wooden bridge was built as part of a realignment of the D&RG to the West side of the river. This was done in concert with Otto Mears' construction of the Rio Grande Southern Railroad and his founding of Ridgway as the home terminal of his new railroad. It was necessary to physically connect the D&RG to the RGS to interchange cars.

The new D&RG line proceeded south along the west side of the river to join the old alignment at Piedmont located on CR 23 a short distance South of CR 3. The old alignment and Uncompahgre River Bridge were torn up for use elsewhere and the right of way deeded to the county for use as a road.

The D&RG continued south into Ouray on what is now County Road 17. The grade went around the north and east sides of Black Lake. Just south of Corbet Creek the railroad served the Wanakah Mill. The railroad went around the mill on a low trestle known as the Mill Trestle. The concrete foundations of the mill can still be seen alongside county Rd 17. A siding on the rail line, just south of the entrance to Whispering Pines, was called the Bachelor Switch because it served the Bachelor mine. Closer to Ouray, the American Nettie Mill and the Grand View Mill also had railroad sidings.

D&RGW bridge over the Uncompahgre River. Ridgway, *Photo by Karl Schaeffer.*

The Ramona Townsite Affair
Jim Pettengill

In the 1880s the Denver & Rio Grande Railroad planned to expand to mining towns near its main line. The railroad completed an initial survey to the Ouray area in late 1881, but due to internal problems, did nothing until 1886.

David Day, the outspoken editor of Ouray's *Solid Muldoon* newspaper, started pushing for a branch line to Ouray in 1882. In May of 1886 the Ouray Board of Trade (who Day usually called the "Bored of Trade") offered the D&RG land to build the line. It appeared to some that the line would have to terminate a short distance north of town for engineering and cost reasons, and Day and other speculators began acquiring land. That summer Day began referring to a new town as the terminus of the railroad. At first he called the town Dayton, for "Day's Town", but it was quickly changed to Helena (to flatter Helen Hunt Jackson, the late wife of then D&RG president William S. Jackson), then to Ramona (to further flatter her memory, as this was the title of her wildly popular novel). The town site was located just north of the existing town of Portland, on the valley floor between today's Ponderosa Village and Cedar Hill Cemetery.

Ouray's business community was outraged. Stopping the railroad at Ramona could kill Ouray. Day reported the instigation of a boycott of the *Muldoon* in June, 1886, and on July 2ⁿᵈ he announced, "As next Sunday will be the 4ᵗʰ, let us not overlook the many advantages offered by Dayton as a business point. It is morally certain to be the terminus of the railroad, and in a few brief months will rank as the metropolis of the great and only San Juan". By the time that the Ramona Townsite Company was established in December 1886, the battle lines were drawn. The City of Ouray even trumped up an order to cut off the *Muldoon's* water supply, which was needed to operate its press, in the interests of water conservation.

The situation between Day and the Ouray businessmen got steadily worse. On July 19, 1887 surveyors finished laying out Main Street in Ramona, and there was a rush to buy lots. On July 21ˢᵗ lumber was hauled in and construction began on several buildings.

The following weekend Day's world turned upside-down. His friend and partner David Moffat, the new president of the D&RG, arrived in town on Sunday, July

24th and met secretly with Ouray businessmen. On Tuesday the 26th, the Board of Trade accepted a deal in which Moffat would build the railroad all the way to Ouray and the town would provide the right-of-way and depot location and grade the right-of-way. Day was furious, as this destroyed his investment in Ramona.

The township company issued refunds to all lot owners. The Ouray Branch was built along the cliffs on the west side of the valley, along what are now County Roads 17 and 23, bypassing the town site. The first passenger train pulled in to Ouray on December 15, 1887.

David Day remained bitter about the Ramona affair for the rest of his life. He retired from the newspaper business in 1906 and sold the Ramona Township and most of his ranch to J. P. Donovan in 1907.

The Ramona affair left many unanswered questions: Why did David Moffat change his mind? As an investor in Ramona, along with several other D&RG officials, he stood to lose money. Was a bribe involved? Who initiated the deal, Moffat or the Board of Trade? After more than 100 years the mysteries remain.

David Frakes Day. *Ouray County Historical Society.*

D&RG/D&RGW – What's in a Name?
Don Paulson

The most famous name in Colorado railroading is arguably the Denver and Rio Grande Western. This railroad provided narrow gauge service to Ouray from 1887 until 1953. The Ouray station and yard were located on the property now occupied by the Four J Trailer Court. The railroad grade between Ouray and Ridgway exists today as County Road 17 and some of County Road 23.

In 1953 the track from Ridgway to Ouray was removed and the track from Montrose to Ridgway was widened from the 36-inch narrow gauge width to the 56.5-inch standard gauge width. The Ridgway branch continued to operate until 1976 when the rails were removed due to construction of the Ridgway Reservoir. Much of the passenger equipment that served Ouray can be seen at the Knott's Berry Farm amusement park in Buena Park, California. D&RGW engine No. 318, the last locomotive used on the Ouray Branch, is being rebuilt and may be operating again at the Colorado Railroad Museum in Golden, Colorado.

The Denver and Rio Grande Railway Company (D&RG) was founded by General William Jackson Palmer in October of 1870. The D&RG was built as a narrow gauge railroad because of Palmer's belief that there would be cost savings in building and operating narrow gauge railroads. A narrow gauge railroad is much cheaper to build particularly in mountain areas. Palmer had spent some time in Wales and had seen narrow gauge railroads operating there. In 1881 Palmer organized the Denver and Rio Grande Western Railway (D&RGW) in Utah to build a narrow gauge line from Salt Lake City eastward to the Utah-Colorado state line to connect with the D&RG.

In 1882 the D&RG leased the D&RGW for 30 years. Early in 1883 Palmer was forced out as President of the D&RG but he kept control of the D&RGW. The D&RG Railway was in receivership from 1884 to 1886 when it was reorganized as the Denver and Rio Grande Railroad. The lease to operate the D&RGW was not continued by the new company and for the next fifteen years different management controlled the two roads. On June 24, 1889 the D&RGW became the Rio Grande Western (RGW).

In 1901 the D&RG purchased Palmer's controlling interest in the RGW and the two railroads were brought together under one management. The RGW ceased to exist as a corporate entity in 1908, becoming part of the D&RG.

On August 1, 1921, as part of reorganization in receivership, the D&RG became the Denver and Rio Grande Western Railroad Company (the second D&RGW), a name it kept for the remainder of its corporate life. The D&RGW boasted of going "Through the Rockies, Not Around Them" (see D&RGW Timetable below). Such storied locations as Black Canyon of the Gunnison, Royal Gorge, Tennessee Pass, Moffat Tunnel and Glenwood Canyon attest to the truth of their slogan.

In 1988 the D&RGW purchased through its parent Rio Grande Industries the Southern Pacific Company and decided to use "Southern Pacific" for the combined company name. In 1996 the Union Pacific purchased the Southern Pacific and thus ended the over 125-year existence of the Colorado railroad founded by Palmer in 1870.

D&RGW timetable, 1948. *Don Paulson Collection.*

Water Tanks on the Narrow Gauge
Don Paulson

Ouray County was served by three railroads in the first half of the 20th century – the Silverton Railroad on Red Mountain, the Rio Grande Southern based in Ridgway and the Denver and Rio Grande Western branch line into Ouray. One hundred years ago the narrow gauge railroad operations in southwestern Colorado employed hundreds of steam locomotives. Many people have ridden behind one of these steam locomotives on the Durango and Silverton Narrow Gauge Railroad

The front of a steam train consisted of the steam engine and the boxy tender connected by a drawbar to the engine. The tender of a steam locomotive carried two important loads - fuel (coal, oil, or wood) and water. The fuel was used to boil the water in the boiler to produce steam to drive the cylinders that turned the wheels of the locomotive. The fuel of choice for the narrow gauge railroads of southwestern Colorado was coal. Most of this coal was supplied from mines west of Durango and north of Gunnison.

The water in the tender was used up much more rapidly than the coal and, thus, water tanks were located along the railroad lines more frequently than fuel stations. For example, the Rio Grande Southern Railroad (RGS) was 162 miles in length and had fifteen water tanks, one for every ten miles of track. In contrast there were only four coal bins for fueling engines on the entire main line. The tenders of narrow gauge steam engines of the early 20th century carried from 2,000-5,000 gallons of water and from two to four tons of coal.

The water tanks on the narrow gauge lines of southwestern Colorado were constructed from a standard design developed by the Denver and Rio Grande Railroad in the late 19th century. They were cylindrical in shape with a conical roof and were held together with a dozen strap bands. They held 50,000 gallons of water. The photo on page 103 shows the Los Pinos water tank on the present day Cumbres and Toltec Scenic Railroad.

The water tanks in towns such as Ridgway were filled directly from city water lines and in some cases, such as in Ouray, a tank was not even necessary with the water spout connected directly to a city water main. However, a spring or creek was used to fill most remote water tanks. If the water source was uphill from the tank, it was kept full by continuous flow of water by gravity. In those cases where the water source was downhill from the tank, a pump was used to fill the tank.

Keeping the water in the tank from freezing in the winter was always a problem. Another serious problem faced by all steam locomotive operations was the poor quality of the water available. If the mineral content of the water was too high, scale would build up on the inside of the boiler causing hot spots, which could result in a boiler explosion. Chemicals were often used to soften the water.

There were several water tanks on the narrow gauge lines in Ouray County. These include RGS tanks at Ridgway and at Valley View on the climb up to Dallas Divide. The Ouray Branch of the D&RGW had a city water spout in Ouray, a tank at Piedmont three miles south of Ridgway and a tank at Cow Creek about one mile north of the present Pa-Co-Chu-Puk entrance to Ridgway State Park.

The D&RGW and the RGS had specialized "Water Service" cars that were used to carry the tools and parts needed to keep the water tanks and their supply pipes operating. These cars were moved from water tank to water tank along the railroad, probably along with a bunk car, and the plumbers and carpenters would have lived at each tank while the needed repairs were being made. The Ridgway Railroad Museum has restored one of these water service cars that is now open to the public.

Los Pinos tank on the Cumbres and Toltec Scenic RR, May, 2008. *Photo by Don Paulson.*

The Last Train from Ouray
Don Paulson

In October of 1952 the Denver and Rio Grande Western (D&RGW) Railroad received permission from the Interstate Commerce Commission to abandon the line between Ridgway and Ouray. The abandonment of the Rio Grande Southern Railroad in 1951 had removed the last need for a narrow gauge connection between Ouray and Montrose. The trackage between Montrose and Ridgway would be standard gauged.

During the fall of 1952 and the following winter, D&RGW section crews used bulldozers to widen the right of way between Montrose and Ridgway and replace the narrow gauge ties with standard gauge ties. By early March the roadbed was ready for widening the track to standard gauge and the little narrow gauge Ouray branch was doomed after more than 60 years of service.

The last train from Ouray left town in a light snow shower late in the afternoon on March 21, 1953 (see photo on page 105). In its March 27th issue, the *Ouray Herald* carried a short article toward the bottom of the front page describing the scene. D&RGW narrow gauge 2-8-0 No. 318 departed with engineer L. S. Braswell at the throttle, as he had been for more than 40 years, along with fireman Frank Wright, conductor John Collett and brakemen Joe Mozza and John Chiodo. The train to Ouray earlier in the day was a "caboose hop" consisting of the engine, tender and caboose. It left Montrose in bright sunlight but the weather deteriorated to a wet spring snow by the time it reached Ouray.

The final out bound trip added three cars of ore concentrates from the Camp Bird Mine, four empty coal gondolas and the two boxcars that had served as the depot after the original depot burned in 1948. The Camp Bird Mine was one of the few loyal shippers to not switch from railroad to truck transport of ore concentrates. The train arrived back in Montrose at 7:28 pm. Fortunately, the 318 was saved from the scrapper's torch in 1954 by Cornelius W. Hauck and is currently located at the Colorado Railroad Museum in Golden.

No one seemed particularly sad about the demise of the narrow gauge. The last regularly scheduled passenger train had left town on September 14, 1930 and even mixed train passenger service ended on July 5, 1936. The March 3, 1953 edition of the

Ouray Herald mentioned how excited the shippers were to get broad gauge train service from Ridgway that would eliminate transfer of goods from narrow gauge to standard gauge cars in Montrose.

Grand Junction Trainmaster Harry Brooks soon had 100 men between Montrose and Ridgway moving the rails out to standard gauge width at the rate of 5 miles per day. In less than a week the tracks were readied for D&RGW GP 7 diesel engines.

The April 3, 1953 issue of the *Ouray Herald* noted the first arrival of a standard gauge diesel freight train in Ridgway. It was 10 hours late because of a broken rail at Kelly's Crossing. Its only paying freight was a gondola of coal destined for Rice Lumber. However, the yards in Ridgway were a beehive of activity as facilities for loading stock, ore concentrates and other merchandise were being newly constructed for standard gauge cars. At the same time the narrow gauge track between Ridgway and Ouray was quickly removed.

The dieselized and standard gauged Ridgway branch survived for another two decades until it too succumbed to low traffic and the Ridgway Reservoir that inundated several miles of its track.

Last Train from Ouray, 1953. *Photo by Bob Richardson, Colorado Railroad Museum.*

Cinders and Smoke on Celluloid: Narrow Gauge in the Movies
Jim Pettengill

The sight of a steam locomotive chugging along a sparkling stream with snow-capped mountains in the background strongly suggests the Old West, so it should be no surprise that southwestern Colorado's narrow gauge railroads were a favorite location for Hollywood's westerns. After World War II, the Denver and Rio Grande Western approached Hollywood filmmakers, and between 1949 and the early seventies, more than a dozen movies were filmed in southwestern Colorado. Most of these featured the D&RGW's Silverton Branch. Some showed the Cumbres and Toltec Scenic Railroad, and a few used railroad artifacts in Ridgway to create the effect of western railroads.

The first of these movies was *Colorado Territory* (1949), followed by *A Ticket to Tomahawk* in 1950. *Tomahawk* was a musical comedy that told of constructing a railroad in 1875. Railfans consider the star of the show to be Rio Grande Southern locomotive No. 20, which was heavily decorated and named the "Emma Sweeney" in the movie. Film buffs remember *Tomahawk* mostly as a very early appearance of Marilyn Monroe. In 1952 *Denver and Rio Grande* featured the first actual crash of two trains in color.

Michael Todd filmed portions of his blockbuster adventure film *Around the World in 80 Days* (1956) in the Durango area. In one dramatic scene, D&RG locomotive No. 315 (which had been retired to display duty in the Durango city park) appears to pull a train that is under attack by hostile Indians through a tunnel while one of the stars races along the roofs of the cars. This scene was filmed at Rockwood Cut north of Durango. The open cut was covered to make the tunnel; locomotive No. 315 was not operative at the time, so a smoke generating device was installed in its firebox and the train was actually pushed by a diesel locomotive disguised as a boxcar! Locomotive 315 has now been completely restored to operating condition and pulled its first passenger train in more than 50 years in September of 2007 (see photo on page 108). The 315 has special significance for southwestern Colorado, as it regularly ran on the Ouray Branch.

Perhaps the best western to show both the Silverton Branch of the D&RGW and the mines around Silverton was *Night Passage* (1957). This film starred James Stewart as an accordion-playing railroad detective charged with recovering a payroll from a gang of thieves led by his brother, the Utica Kid, played by Audie Murphy. Along with spectacular railroad footage, there is a great shootout at the Mayflower Mill located just northeast of Silverton.

Perhaps the most ambitious Western ever filmed, *How the West Was Won* (1962) followed the story of four generations of a family as they moved west. Part of this movie was filmed in Ridgway, where the Ridgway Depot building was dressed up as the Independence, Missouri Hotel. In 1969, *True Grit* was filmed in Ouray County, and RGS caboose 400 was shown, with steam and smoke blowing into view to suggest a railroad, even though most signs of the RGS were long gone by then. RGS caboose No. 400 is currently at the Colorado Railroad Museum in Golden.

One of the most memorable scenes in any western came from *Butch Cassidy and the Sundance Kid* (1969). After the Wild Bunch blow up the baggage car, which actually happened in Wilcox, Wyoming ("Think you used enough dynamite, Butch?"), a sinister-looking locomotive arrives on the scene pulling a baggage car, which opens and disgorges a mounted posse. This prompts the line "Who are those guys?" That baggage car (built especially for the film) was formerly on display at the Ridgway Railroad Museum and is now on private property at the corner of Amelia Street and County Road 5 in Ridgway.

Among the other movies filmed on the D&RGW were *Across the Wide Missouri* (1951), *Viva Zapata!* (1952), *Three Young Texans* (1954), *Run for Cover* (1955), *Maverick Queen* (1956), and *Support Your Local Gunfighter* (1971).

D&RGW No. 315 on the High Line north of Rockwood, Colorado, September 2008. *Photo by Jim Pettengill.*

Bibliography

Athearn, R., *The Denver and Rio Grande Western Railroad*, University of Nebraska Press, Lincoln, NE, 1977.

Chappell, G., "Train Time in Ouray," in *Colorado Rail Annual No. 11*, Hauck, C. W., Ed., Colorado Railroad Museum, Golden, CO, 1973.

Coleman, Ross, McCoy, Dell A., *et. al. The RGS Story*, Volumes I-XII, Sundance Publications, Denver, CO, 1990-2006.

Crum, J. M., *The Rio Grande Southern Railroad*, San Juan History, Inc., Durango, CO, 1961.

Crum, J. M., *Three Little Lines*. Durango Herald News, Durango, CO, 1960.

Dorman, R. L., *The Rio Grande Southern: An Ultimate Pictorial Study*, RD Publications, Santa Fe, NM, 1990.

Dorman, R. L., *The Rio Grande Southern II: An Ultimate Pictorial Study*, RD Publications, Santa Fe, NM, 1994.

Ehernberger, J. L., *Sunset on the Rio Grande Southern, Vol 1*, Challenger Press, Cheyene, WY, 1996.

Ehernberger, J. L., *Sunset on the Rio Grande Southern, Vol 2*, Challenger Press, Cheyene, WY, 1996.

Ferrell, M. H., *Silver San Juan*, Pruett Publishing Co., Boulder, CO, 1973.

Ferrell, M. H., *Narrow Gauge Country*, Heimburger House Publishing, Forest Park, IL, 2006.

Gregory, D. H., *History of Ouray*, Vol. I, Cascade Publications, Ouray, CO, 1995.

Gregory, D. H., *History of Ouray*, Vol. II Cascade Publications, Ouray, CO, 1997.

Gregory, D. H., *The Town that Refused to Die, Ridgway, Colorado, 1890-1991*, Cascade Publications, Ouray, CO, 1992.

Ingersoll, E., *Crest of the Continent*, Lakeside Press, Chicago, IL, 1885

Jocknick, S., *Early Days on the Western Slope of Colorado*, Western Reflections Publishing Co., Ouray, CO, 1998.

Kaplan, M., *Otto Mears Paradoxical Pathfinder*, San Juan Book Co., Silverton, CO, 1982.

Lathrop, Gilbert, *Little Engines and Big Men*, Caxton Printers, Caldwell, ID, 1955.

LeMassena, R. A., *Rio Grande to the Pacific*, Sundance Limited, Denver, CO, 1974.

Niebur, J. E.; Fell, Jr., J. E., *Arthur Redman Wilfley*, Colorado Historical Society, Denver, CO, 1982.

Osterwald, D. E., *Cinders & Smoke: a Mile-by-Mile Guide for the Durango to Silverton Narrow Gauge Trip*, Western Guideways, Lakewood, CO, 1968.

Rhine, S., "Galloping Geese on the Rio Grande Southern: Tin Feathers and Gasoline Fumes," in *Colorado Rail Annual No. 9*, Hauck, C. W., Ed., Colorado Railroad Museum, Golden, CO, 1971.

Rice, F. A., *The Mines of Ouray County*, Bear Creek Publishing Co., Ouray, CO, 1980.

Ridgway Railroad Museum, *Selected Primary Source Materials from the Museum Archives*, Ridgway, CO.

Ripley, Henry; Ripley, M., *Hand-Clasp of the East and West*, Williams-Haffner Engraving and Printing Co., Denver, CO, 1914.

Sloan, R. E., *A Century + Ten of D&RGW Narrow Gauge Freight Cars, 1871 to 1981,* BHI Publications, Cottleville, MO, 2003.

Sloan, R. E.; Skowronski, A., *The Rainbow Route*, Sundance Publications, Silverton, CO, 1975.

Smith, P. D., *Exploring the Historic San Juan Triangle*, Wayfinder Press, Ridgway, CO, 2004.

Smith, P. D., *Mountains of Silver*, Pruett Publishing Co., Boulder, CO, 1994.

Strong, W. K., *The Remarkable Railroad Passes of Otto Mears*, San Juan Book Co., Silverton, CO, 1988.

Tucker, E. F., *Otto Mears and the San Juans*, Western Reflections Publishing Co., Montrose, CO, 2003.

Twitty, E., *Basins of Silver*, Western Reflections Publishing Co., Lake City, CO, 2008.

Wolle, M. S., *Stampede to Timberline*, Sage Books, Chicago, IL, 1949.

Wolle, M. S., *Timberline Tailings*, Sage Books, Chicago, IL, 1977.

Made in the USA
Columbia, SC
25 September 2020